Copyright

Copyright © 2016 by D

All rights reserved

Disclaimer

Command line and batch script can affect your computer system(s) and the data stored on it/them. It is advisable to learn these skills in a test environment, such as on a virtual machine. It is possible to download virtual machine software for free online, such as Oracle VM VirtualBox. It is also advisable to back up any data to a separate storage device, such as a USB pen drive, or to cloud storage, before running any commands.

While the advice and information in this book are believed to be true and accurate at the date of publication, neither the author nor the publisher can accept any legal responsibility for any errors or omissions that may be made. The publisher and author makes no warranty, express or implied, with respect to the material contained herein.

Table of Contents – All Volumes

- Copyright 1
- Disclaimer 2
- Table of Contents – All Volumes 3
- Volume 1 21
  - Introduction 22
    - Progression 22
    - Technical terms 22
    - Formatting 23
    - Modules 23
    - Exercises and Answers 23
    - Getting started 23
  - Basic Information Commands 25
    - Hostname 25
    - Ver 26
    - Vol 26
  - Detailed information commands 28
    - IPConfig 28
    - Systeminfo 29
    - Help 30
  - Customising the console 32
    - Title 32
    - Prompt 33
    - Exercise - Your Version 33
    - Color 33

3

- Exercise - Colour Codes 34
- Cls 34
- Pause 35

Batch files 36
- Scripts vs. Programs vs. Code 36
- Making and editing batch files 37
- Running batch files 37
  - Exercise – customise the console (custom.bat) 38
- Running programs 38

Comments 40
- Rem 40

File system info 41
- Dir 41
- Tree 43

Navigation 44
- Chdir (Cd) 44
  - Exercise – go to your batch folder (custom2.bat) 46

Reading, writing and redirecting text 47
- Test folders 47
- Type 47
- Echo 48
  - The command 48
  - Following up 49
  - Exercise – two new lines (twoLines.bat) 50
  - Escape characters 50
  - Redirection operators 50

Exercise – clear a file (clearFile.bat) 51
Exercise – redirect information (sysInfo.bat) 51
Exercise – collect information (gather.bat) 52
More on redirection 52
The pipe operator 52
Turning echo on and off 53
Handles 54
Using parameters in your batch scripts 55
Exercise – back up a file (backup.bat) 56

Other actions 57
Chkdsk 57
Shutdown 58
Ping 59
Timeout 61
Runas 61

Variables 62
Set 62
The command 63
Naming your variables 64
Accepting user input 64
Exercise – log user input (logIn.bat) 65
Exercise – log command output (logOut.bat) 65
Exercise – log errors (logErr.bat) 65
Processing numbers 65
Numbers and networks 66
Shorthand number processing 66

Exercise - find the remainder (mod.bat) 67
Exercise – division (divideA.bat) 67
Exercise – square a number (square.bat) 67
Processing strings 67
Processing substrings by position 67
Processing substrings by content 69
Stored commands 69
Exercises 70
Exercise – make an IP address (getIP.bat) 70
Exercise – left (left10.bat) 70
Exercise – right (right10.bat) 70
Exercise – middle (char3.bat) 70
Exercise – replace (trim.bat) 70
Exercise – Americanise (UKtoUS.bat) 71
Goto 71
Exercise – messenger (writer.bat, reader.bat, flush.bat) 71
Exercise – security (writer2.bat) 72
Decisions 73
If 73
Using 'if' with 'else', 'not', and 'exist' 73
Comparing strings 75
A neat trick 75
Case-sensitivity 76
Comparing numbers 77
Making your script more reliable 77
Handling errors 78

Exercise – check a file exists (isHere.bat) 78
Exercise – infinity (divideB.bat) 78
Exercise – absolute (absA.bat, absB.bat) 78
Exercise – command selector (info.bat) 78
Exercise – validation (info2.bat) 78

Volume 2 79

Introduction 80

Naming System 80

Organisation 80

Command syntax 81

File Contents and Filtering 82

More 83

Displaying command output: the basics 83

Displaying command output: extras 83

File reading basics 84

File reading extras 84

Exercise – quickly reading through files (scanLogs.bat) 85

Sort 85

Sort: the basics 86

Exercise – sort inside files (sortFile.bat) 86

Exercise – the '/r' switch (sortFileR.bat) 86

Sort: from here on in 86

Performance issues 87

Find 88

Find: the basics 88

Find: the other switches 89

7

Exercise – combining switches (mismatchTotal.bat) 89
Find: extras 89
Exercise – searching command output (bootTime.bat) 89
Findstr 90
Findstr: the basics 90
Findstr: position switches 90
Exercise: searching command output better (justOS.bat) .. 91
Findstr: the switches from 'find' 91
Findstr: the detail switches 91
Findstr: searching for alternatives 92
Findstr: getting parameters from files 92
Findstr: subdirectories 92
Findstr: finding multiple words together 93
Findstr: regex switches 93
Regex: repeated and optional characters 93
Exercise – optional characters (commas.bat) 93
Regex: wildcards 94
Exercise – repeated wildcards (twoWords.bat) 94
Regex: word position options 94
Exercise – endings (ending.bat) 94
Exercise – beginnings (beginning.bat) 95
Regex: character classes and ranges 95
Exercise –ranges (endInDigit.bat, endIn1Digit.bat) 95
Exercise – numbers only (zipCode.bat) 95
Exercise – labels only (labelsOnly.bat) 95
Regex: taking characters literally 96

Exercise – escaping (getCSVs.bat) 96
Regex: why use the R switch? 96
Exercise – A tricky end (trickyEnd.bat) 97
Conclusion 97
FC 97
FC: the basics 98
FC: comparison switches 98
FC: re-synchronising switches 100
Comp 101
Comp: the basics 101
Comp: files of different sizes 103

Changing course in a script 104
Goto 104
Goto: skipping steps 105
Goto: choosing from two options 106
Goto: choosing from multiple options 107
Goto: looping 108
Exercise – checking for user input (checkInput.bat) 109
Exercise – making dummy files (makeDummy.bat) 109

More about variables 111
Setlocal 111
Setlocal: parameters 113
Normal expansion 113
Delayed expansion 114
Working with strings 115
Endlocal 115

9

Exercise – a string replace 'function' (stringReplace.bat) .. 116

Exercise – make dummy files differently (makeDummy2.bat) 116

Knowing when to quit 117

Exit 117

The need for 'exit' 117

Exiting 118

Exiting just the script 119

Exit codes: how they work 119

Error codes: why they matter 120

Error levels and 'if' 121

File and Folder operations 122

Del 122

Del: the basics 123

Deleting from subdirectories 123

Deleting read-only and hidden files 124

Deleting files with certain attributes 125

Rename (ren) 125

Ren: the basics 125

Ren: wildcards 126

Ren: file extensions 127

Ren: renaming folders 127

Exercise – restore a file from backup (restore.bat) 127

Exercise – safely restore a file from backup (safeRestore.bat) 128

Call: a brief introduction 128

10

    Exercise – return error messages for exit codes (parent.bat) 129

  MkDir 129

    Exercise – make folders differently (mkdirs.bat) 130

  Rmdir (rd) 130

  Move 131

    Moving folders 131

    Renaming folders 131

    Prompt switches 132

    Exercise – restore a folder from backup (restoreDir.bat) . 132

  Attrib 132

    Attrib: the basics 133

    Read-only 133

    Hidden files 134

    Removing attributes 135

    Attrib: without file names and with wildcards 135

    Attrib: subfolders 135

    Exercise – Clearing attributes (clearAll.bat) 135

Copying files and folders 136

  Copy 136

    Copy: the basics 136

    Exercise – new name, new folder (myCopy.bat) 137

    Overwriting and prompting 137

    Consolidating files 137

    Copying multiple files 137

    Question 138

  Answer 138

  Exercise – backup multiple files (backup.bat) 138

  Exercise – restore multiple files (restoreAll.bat) 138

  Exercise – safely restore multiple files (safeRestoreAll.bat)
  138

 Replace 138

  Replace: the basics 139

  Replace: subfolders 139

  Replace: adding files 140

  Replace: updating files 140

  Other switches 141

 Xcopy 141

  XCopy: introduction 141

  XCopy: prompt switches 142

  XCopy: folder switches 143

  XCopy: file attribute switches 144

  Exercise – back up a folder (backupDir.bat) 146

Volume 3 147

 Introduction 148

  Naming System 148

  Command syntax 148

 Navigating networks 149

  Explorer 149

 Virtual Drives 151

  Subst 151

   Note 151

Mapping a drive on your own computer 152
Drives within drives 152
Deleting virtual drives 153
Mapping a drive over a network 153
Uses 153
Exercise – copying across a network (copyToMap.bat) 154
Pushd 154
Popd 155
Subroutines 157
Call 157
Running other scripts and programs 158
Calling another batch file as a subroutine 159
Exercise – getting an IP address (logMe.bat, callLogMe.bat)
.... 160
Calling subroutines in the same batch file 160
Making functions 162
The problem with variables 163
The problem with local variables 164
Beating 'setlocal' and 'endlocal' 164
Variable modifiers... 166
Exercise – getting information about other files (fileInfo.bat)
.... 167
Independent subroutines.. 168
Start.. 168
Working in parallel 168
Exercise – delaying tactics (doProcess.bat, getData.bat)... 170

13

- Keeping control 170
- Exercise – the simple fix (doProcess2.bat, getData2.bat).. 171
- Exercise – the checkpoint solution (doProcess3.bat, getData3.bat) 171
- Other information 171

Checking, and stopping, other programs 172
- Tasklist 172
  - The basics 172
  - Extra detail 173
  - Cutting down.. 173
  - Exercise – using filters (listServices.bat)...................... 174
  - Formatting 174
  - Networks.. 174
  - Exercise – Detective work (getImageName.bat)................ 174
- Taskkill... 175
  - Exercise – Excel yourself (closeExcel.bat)..................... 177

Using loops on almost anything 178
- For 178
  - Overview 178
  - Using 'for' in the command line 179
  - Using 'for' in batch script 180
  - Defining your set.. 180
  - Making changes 180
  - Exercise – read and write (raw.bat)............................. 181
  - Exercise – make a list (list.bat) 181
  - Exercise – one loop, two commands (list2.bat)................ 181

Variable modifiers 181

Folder switch: /d 182

Subfolder switch: /r 182

Number switch: /l 183

Exercise – make IPs (makeIPs.bat) 184

Arrays 184

Setting variables with delayed expansion 185

Exercise – running total (countFiles.bat) 186

Exercise – stopping part way (top3.bat) 186

Text switch: /f 186

Getting 'words' 187

Getting columns 187

Exercise – using tokens (getColumn3.bat) 188

Getting lines 188

Exercise – one-liners (get1Line.bat) 189

Exercise – better one-liners (getLineNum.bat) 190

Exercise – even better one-liners (getAnyLineNum.bat) ... 190

Exercise – find a value (getValue.bat) 190

Multiple columns 190

Exercise – re-using those variables (reverse.bat) 191

Exercise – turn the tables (columnSwap.bat) 191

Implications 191

Variable numbers of columns 192

Comment characters 192

Usebackq – File names with spaces in 193

Looping through strings 194

    Looping through command output 195

    Setting variables from text 196

    Loops, pipes, and subroutines 196

    Exercise – find and replace, a primer (lineReplace1.bat) .. 197

    Exercise – find and replace, the real deal (mainReplace2.bat, lineReplace2.bat) 198

Dealing with unknown numbers of parameters 199

    Shift 199

        Using parameters 199

        The zero parameter 199

        Exercise – unintended consequences 200

        Exercise – escape the consequences (get0.bat) 200

        The other parameters 200

        Using 'shift' 201

        Switch usage 202

        Exercise – minimal effort (easyShifter.bat) 202

        Exercise – doing a better job of it (shifter.bat) 202

        The everything parameter 202

        Exercise – log everything (asterisk.bat) 203

Conclusion - where to go from here 204

    Warning 204

    Installing programs 204

    Managing Windows systems 204

    PSTools 205

    Managing disks 205

    Managing services 205

Net commands	206
More commands	206
Author's Note	207
You've finished. Before you go…	208
More by this author	208
Answers – Volume 1	209
absA.bat	209
absB.bat	209
backup.bat	209
char3.bat	209
clearFile.bat	210
Colour Codes	210
custom.bat	210
custom2.bat	210
divideA.bat	210
divideB.bat	210
flush.bat	211
gather.bat	211
getIP.bat	211
info.bat	212
info2.bat	212
isHere.bat	213
left10.bat	213
logErr.bat	214
logIn.bat	215
logOut.bat	215

17

- mod.bat 215
- reader.bat 215
- right10.bat 216
- square.bat 216
- sysInfo.bat 216
- trim.bat 216
- twoLines.bat 216
- UKtoUS.bat 216
- writer.bat 217
- writer2.bat 217
- Your Version 217

Answers – Volume 2 218
- backup.bat 218
- backupDir.bat 218
- beginning.bat 218
- bootTime.bat 218
- checkInput.bat 218
- clearAll.bat 218
- commas.bat 219
- endIn1Digit.bat 219
- endInDigit.bat 219
- ending.bat 219
- getCSVs.bat 219
- justOS.bat 219
- labelsOnly.bat 220
- makeDummy.bat 220

makeDummy2.bat 221

mismatchTotal.bat 222

mkdirs.bat 222

myCopy.bat 223

parent.bat 223

restore.bat 224

restoreAll.bat 224

restoreDir.bat 224

safeRestore.bat 224

safeRestoreAll.bat 224

scanLogs.bat 225

sortFile.bat 225

sortFileR.bat 225

stringReplace.bat 225

trickyEnd.bat 225

twoWords.bat 225

zipCode.bat 226

Answers – Volume 3 227

asterisk.bat 227

callLogMe.bat 227

closeExcel.bat 227

columnSwap.bat 227

copyToMap.bat 227

countFiles.bat 228

doProcess.bat 228

doProcess2.bat 229

19

doProcess3.bat 229

easyShifter.bat 229

fileInfo.bat 230

get0.bat 230

get1Line.bat 231

getAnyLineNum.bat 231

getColumn3.bat 231

getData.bat 232

getData2.bat 232

getData3.bat 232

getImageName.bat 232

getLineNum.bat 233

getValue.bat 233

lineReplace1.bat 234

lineReplace2.bat 234

list.bat 234

list2.bat 234

listServices.bat 234

logMe.bat 235

mainReplace2.bat 235

makeIPs.bat 235

raw.bat 235

reverse.bat 235

shifter.bat 236

top3.bat 236

20

Volume 1

Introduction

Welcome to Learn Command Line and Batch Scripting Fast, Volume 1! The command line is a means of controlling Windows systems. Batch script is a means of automating what you do with the command line. Together they provide powerful tools for IT support workers, system administrators, and anyone who wants to perform, or have their computer perform, routine tasks more efficiently.

This book is part one of a three part course for people who want to learn how to use command line, write batch scripts, or both. It is designed to cover as much as possible, as concisely as possible, with plenty of examples and practice exercises.

Running your first command can be as simple as typing the command name and pressing 'enter'. The first chapter covers a few examples just like that.

Before that, here are some notes on how to use this book.

Progression
All sections teach basic commands and any related concepts, and include examples. Later sections also show how to combine their commands with those covered earlier. They include exercises to provide practice doing this, by making batch scripts. These use the same commands.

Technical terms
Technical or specialist terms (jargon) are either defined before use, or introduced in brackets (parentheses) after a plain English equivalent.

Formatting

Sometimes, a command is too long to fit on one line of the page, but should still be typed as one line on your computer. These commands are formatted as shown in example one, below.

1) This is how one command spread over two lines on the page looks: note that its lines are close together.

2) Note the wider space between this line and the lines above. This is how a separate command looks.

Modules

Each section, whether a command, exercise, chapter, or book, is designed to be as self-contained as possible. This is to make it easy to refer back to them. However, the sections and exercises have been ordered to introduce topics step-by-step.

Exercises and Answers

This book includes practice exercises.

The batch scripts which form the answers to these exercises can be found at the back of the book. Each exercise is followed by the name of the batch script file, or similar, which solves it; so you can find that script, or command, in the answers and compare it to your own solution.

Even if you are completely satisfied with your own solution, it is still worth checking the answers to see if there is an alternative solution that you can learn from.

The exercises start in chapter three, 'Customising the Console'.

Getting started

The first thing you need is Microsoft Windows. The next thing you need is an open command window. If you have Windows 8, or newer, bring up the 'search' option, type 'cmd', and click on the result. If you have an older version of Windows, open the start menu on your desktop, click the 'run' option, type 'cmd' and press 'enter' on your keyboard. You will now have an open command window.

The window will contain some text, followed by a '_' character blinking on and off. This text is the command prompt, where you can type commands in, before pressing 'enter' to run them. You may also come across the terms 'command line' or 'cmd line', but no matter the term used, your starting point is the one described here.

Basic Information Commands

Using command line can be very simple. Sometimes, it's as simple as typing a few letters and pressing enter. Sometimes, commands simply provide a way to check information about a computer. Often, they are the fastest and simplest way to do so.

This chapter introduces some of those commands.

You type a command, press 'enter', and the computer tells you things. Things like:

What is the computer's name (on your network)?

What version of Windows does it use?

What are the details of a specified volume, e.g. on the hard disk of the C: drive?

The commands are 'hostname', 'ver' and 'vol'. Try them out, as shown below.

Hostname

What it does: gets and displays the name of the host machine (your computer, in this case)

Why use it: for information

How to use it:

Run 'hostname' (type 'hostname' into the command window and press 'enter') on a computer to see its name on your network.

This comes in useful later in this book, when covering how to work with remote computers (networked computers which you control indirectly, via your own machine). For example, you can use the hostname to test if a machine is running on your network, or to connect to that machine and work on it.

Ver

What it does: displays the version of Windows being used

Why use it: for information

How to use it:

Run 'ver' to see your version of Windows.

Vol

What it does: displays the name and serial number of the volume (this usually corresponds to a physical hard disk in home PCs) in the current drive, e.g. 'volume in drive C is Windows, serial number 12345'

Why use it: for information

How to use it:

Run 'vol' to see your disk volume label and serial number. These will be the details for the volume in your current drive, which is usually the C drive: 'C:'. Your computer may only have one drive, although you could attach a USB, or a Kindle, and 'vol' could report on that.

To run the command on another drive, you can change to that drive first. For example, if you have a D drive, type 'D:' and press enter. If you don't know what drives you have, just try a few different letters. You will see the text 'D:\>' appear in the command window. This text (the command prompt) indicates where your command will run, unless you specify otherwise. Run 'vol' again. You will see a different result. Run 'C:' (or whichever letter you started with) to return to the C drive.

Also, you can input the drive name directly into the command, e.g. by running 'vol D:'. Try that now. Information added like this, after a command, is called a parameter. Parameters are separated from commands, and from each other, by spaces.

Sometimes, you will want to use a parameter which has a space in it. In these cases, you will need to put double-quotes around the parameter, so the command line knows it is a single unit.

Note: if you type quotes into the command window, they will appear as (very short) straight lines, and will work. If you copy and paste them in, from Word for example, you may end up with curly quotes, which don't work.

Detailed information commands

While a few commands provide specific information, others provide more detail. They are used the same way: type the command name and press enter. The main difference is that they provide large blocks: lists, tables, or pages of information.

They can, for example, provide details of your computer's network settings (configuration), information about your computer system, or pages of instructions for using commands.

Some of these commands also provide switches or parameters to help handle the larger blocks of information they display. Should these not be enough, books two and three provide additional ways to handle large amounts of text.

Some commands of this type are 'ipconfig', 'systeminfo', and 'help'.

IPConfig

What it does: displays information about the network settings (IP configuration) of the machine

Why use it: to see any of those details

How to use it:

Run 'ipconfig'. You will see a list of details. One of these will be the IP address, or IPv4 address. This is made up of four groups of numbers separated by '.' characters. It identifies your computer, or device, on a network. This may be your home or office network. If you know a computer's IP address, you can connect to it from another machine on the network (i.e. remotely). This allows you to run commands on other machines, e.g. shut one down, or interact with it, e.g. transfer files to or from it.

Run 'ipconfig /all'. You will see even more details than before. The '/all' on the end of your command caused the extras bits to appear. The '/all' part is known as a switch. Switches change how commands work. Like parameters, they are separated by spaces. Unlike parameters, they are marked by beginning with a '/' character (called 'slash' or 'forward slash') although some switches begin with a '-' character instead. It does not matter what case your switch is: '/all' does the same thing as '/ALL'.

Switches are individual to commands, if you use 'ver /all', for example, you just get an error. However, commands often have switches with the same names, to do the same, or similar, things. For example, all commands can be followed by the help switch '/?'. This displays the help information for the command.

Some of the switches listed in the help for 'ipconfig' take the command beyond displaying information, and actually make it change network settings, but those are not part of this course.

Systeminfo

What it does: displays information about the operating system (OS)

Why use it: to see any of those OS details

How to use it:

Run 'systeminfo'. You will see a lot of information, including a long list of updates, or 'fixes'. Have a look through and see the kinds of information you can find out. For example, if you want to know when the computer was turned on (booted), you would look for the 'system boot time', or a similar phrase, depending on your computer. You can see information about a computer's time zone, available memory, and so on.

Now run 'systeminfo /?'. You will see the help information for the command. The help starts with the command name, followed by the switches and parameters that can be used with it. In the help, these are separated from the command with square brackets '[]' meaning they are optional to it. However, you will notice that some of the switches and parameters are separated only by spaces, not brackets. This means they are pairs, to be used together. For example, '/S' should be followed by the 'system' parameter, the IP address of a computer on your network. Another switch, '/FO', is meant to be followed by a format parameter, such as the word 'table'. You can read down the help, to see more details about how to use the command. You can use the help switch to find out which switches and parameters you can use with each new command you see.

To get information about other computers on a network, you would use '/S'. But even if you don't have a network, you can still try out the '/S' switch. Use the IP address you get from 'ipconfig'. If it is, for example, 10.20.30.40, run 'systeminfo /s 10.20.30.40' and your computer will find itself on the network, and return results.

Try out 'systeminfo /fo csv'. Whereas before you had a list, you will now see two paragraphs. Each paragraph contains one column of the list, with the 'rows' now separated by commas. CSV stands for Comma Separated Values. This format is less readable, but perfect for if you want to copy the information into a spreadsheet or database. You could even copy it to a '.csv' file, which opens in Excel with each 'value' in its own square (cell) on the grid, and the separating commas removed. This topic is covered in more depth later in the course.

Help

What it does: Displays help information in the command window.

Why use it: To read up on how the command line works.

How to use it:

Run 'help' to see general help information in the command window.

To see help for a particular command, run the command name with the '/?' switch, e.g. 'ver /?'.

Alternatively, type 'help' with the command name as a parameter, e.g. 'help ver'.

One thing you will see often, in the help text of many commands, is the phrase 'if command extensions are enabled' followed by a list of extra things the command can do. Command extensions are enabled by default, so just assume you can use any such extras for now. Later in this course, you will learn how to enable and disable command extensions. There is a command for it!

Customising the console

It's time for some commands that change settings. This chapter shows how to customise what the console (command window) displays. This includes setting the text of the title and prompt and setting the colour of the text and background. It covers how to clear the screen of unwanted text and also how to pause a command sequence to give users time to see any results.

The commands customise your command window. They also allow you to have any batch scripts you create customise their own command windows. You can title, or colour-code them, and generally make them more user-friendly and presentable.

The changes are temporary. The command window will return to its usual appearance next time you open it.

The commands are 'title', 'prompt', 'color', 'cls' and 'pause'.

Title
What it does: changes the title (the text in the bar at the top of the command window)

Why use it: to say what a command window is being used for, e.g. which batch script is running on it

How to use it:

Run 'title your wish is my command'. Now spot where the text has appeared in the command window, hint: look up.

Using 'title' changes the title of the command prompt window to whatever you choose. It is useful when running batch script files, to make the command window show which script is running. This is especially true if there is more than one command window open at a time.

Prompt

What it does: customises the command prompt to different characters or information

Why use it: to provide the user with extra information, keeping it visible and up-to-date on screen as each new command is run

How to use it:

The command prompt is the text to the left of where you usually type your commands.

Run 'prompt enter command here: '. The command prompt changes to your text, i.e. 'enter command here:'.

Run 'prompt ds$t'. The command prompt now gives you different information. $D is for date; $T is for time; and $S is for space.

This new command prompt ends rather abruptly. You can use 'prompt' to give it a more appropriate ending, like '>'. Run 'prompt dstg'. Then, to set the prompt back to the default, run 'prompt', without parameters.

Finally, run 'prompt /?' to see the other types of information that the command prompt can display.

Exercise - Your Version
Use the help information to make the command prompt display the version of Windows your machine is running, followed by a '>' character and a space.

Color

What it does: changes the colour of the text or background in the command window

Why use it: several reasons, see below

How to use it: Run 'color 2' then 'color a' then 'color b1'.

'Color' lets you customise the command window, both the text and the background colour.

Using one colour value will change the text. Using two, the first value will change the background, the second the text. The colour values are from 0-9 then A-F (in place of 10-15). Run 'Color /?' to see what they all are.

Now run 'color' to restore the original colour scheme of the command window.

There are several reasons to use 'color'. It can make it easier to read a window's text. It can highlight a change: such as completion of a batch script or an error occurring. You could have the screen change to green or red in those cases, and be alerted to its finishing from the other end of the office. If you have several batch script windows running at once, it can also help distinguish them. You can colour command windows differently, to help users see they are on the correct one more easily.

Exercise - Colour Codes
Can you make the command window blue with white text?

Cls
What it does: clears the screen of the command window

Why use it: to keep the command prompt window clear of old information, making it tidier and easier to read

How to use it:

Type something, e.g. 'ipconfig', into the command window, and after running the command, run 'cls'. The command window is suddenly clear. CLS clears the screen.

Pause

What it does: stops a batch script from running until the user presses a key

Why use it: to allow the user to time to read output and decide whether to proceed

How to use it:

Normally, you would use 'pause' in a batch script. You can run it in the command window to see how it works. Type 'pause' and press enter. Press another key to finish the command.

Batch files

One of the most powerful features of the command line is its ability to run batch scripts. A batch script is a stored sequence of commands. The sequence can be run as if it were one command. In this way, batch scripts allow more complex tasks to be automated.

The sequence of commands is stored in a batch file. Opening the batch file runs it, by default, executing the commands in the script. The system knows to run the text inside the file as a series of batch commands, because the file's '.bat' extension marks it out as a batch file, to be opened with the command window, rather than notepad, or another text-editing application.

As an example of a script, you could type the command sequence below into a batch file. If you then ran this script, it would change the command window colour scheme, wait for the user to press a key, and then reset those colours.

    COLOR 03

    PAUSE

    COLOR

Scripts vs. Programs vs. Code

This book will generally refer to the contents of a batch file as a 'script'. Occasionally, it may refer to 'programs' or 'programming'. There are some differences in the meaning of 'script' and 'program'. However, for the purposes of this course, you can think of a script as being a specialised type of program.

You may also see the term 'program' used to describe applications like 'Word' or 'Notepad'.

The book may also refer to 'code'. This refers to the contents of a script: the commands. For example, the colour-changing program above contains three lines of code.

Making and editing batch files

There are several ways to make a batch file.

Number one: open Notepad, in the same way you open any application on your computer. Type your script in (e.g. the commands above). Use the 'save as' option. In the 'save as' dialog box, change the 'save as type' dropdown to 'All Files'. Type the name of your batch file in the 'File Name' box, including the '.bat' ending (e.g. 'my1stBatch.bat'), and save. If you need to edit the file later, right-click on it and select **'edit'**, not 'open', from the context menu. If you 'open' a batch file, you run it.

Number two: in Windows Explorer, right-click so that the context menu appears. On it, select the option for 'New', then 'Text Document'. Open the text document that appears. Proceed as you did in the method above.

Number three: in command prompt, run 'notepad my1stBatch.bat'. This creates a batch file called 'my1stBatch' with the correct extension, '.bat', and opens it in notepad. If you re-run that line later, it re-opens the file you created, ready for editing. Type the script above into Notepad. Save the file.

If you use methods one and three above, without changing the file extension to '.bat', you can create text files instead. That will be useful later, when you need dummy files to run commands on.

Running batch files

If you use the command line method, number three, to make your batch file, it is created in the folder shown on your command prompt. Type 'my1stBatch' into the command line and press enter. Your script will now run. Congratulations.

If you use the other two methods, you probably created the batch file in another folder. Go to that folder in the file system (Windows Explorer), and double-click the batch file to run the script. If you do that, your computer will run the script, opening and closing the command window for you at the beginning and end. This means that if you want to see the end result, you need to put 'pause' at the bottom of the script, or the script will run the last command and close straightaway.

Exercise – customise the console (custom.bat)

Design a batch script to turn your command window a different colour and give it a different title. Then have it clear the command window, so the text from your commands doesn't clutter it up. Have it stop at the end, so you can see the result even if you run it from Windows Explorer.

Running programs

Earlier you saw that by typing 'notepad' into command line, you could open it. Likewise, type the name of other programs, applications or files and you can open or run them too. Run 'notepad'. Run 'explorer'.

You also already ran a batch script from the command prompt. Normally, you can only run a batch script if the path (drive and folder) in the command prompt matches the path of the batch file (its drive and folder). If you created and ran the batch script above using the command prompt, it worked because its file was in the same folder as the command prompt was using. You ran notepad from that prompt's path, and then ran the batch file from the same path.

Other files can be opened in a similar way. If you have a file stored in the same folder, called, for example 'myWordFile.docx', you can open it by typing its name with the file extension, and pressing 'enter'.

38

You can run a batch file stored in a different folder by typing the whole path, including the batch file's name at the end. If this contains spaces, you may also need to enclose it in double-quotes.

Alternatively, you can change folder (change directory) to wherever the batch file is stored. That way, the command prompt's path matches the file's location, and you can once again run the file by name alone. The command to change directory will be covered shortly.

Comments

When you write a batch script, you may want to include notes (comments) about what it does. If the system runs your notes as commands, this causes errors. So you need a way to tell the system which lines are not code.

This chapter is about comments, and how to use them.

Rem

What it does: stops the system trying to run a line of text as code

Why use it: to add notes to your code, in plain English, to label what each part of it does

How to use it:

Run 'rem this is a comment'. It does absolutely nothing. This is what it is meant to do. In the command line this has no purpose, but in batch scripts this allows you to include lines which the system will not try to run as commands. Using 'rem' flags those lines as remarks, or comments, rather than commands.

This is a useful for two things. It lets you write plain English notes into the batch file, to say, for example, what the script or parts of the script are meant to do. It also lets you make lines of batch code inactive without deleting them. If you want to test your script without a certain line or section, you can 'comment out' the lines by typing 'rem' in front of them. This makes the program skip them, as if they were deleted, but saves you having to re-type them if the test shows that you do need them after all.

You can also use '::' (two colons) at the start of a line of batch script. The effect is the same.

File system info

A common use of batch scripting is to change the contents of the file system. You can create, read, write, modify, copy, rename or delete files. You can also change the folder structure that holds them. However, to do all this, you need some idea of what you are changing.

This chapter is about that. It covers commands for viewing the file system.

If you want to see the contents of a folder, a map of subfolders, or the properties of files, there are commands for these.

If you want to move around the file system, as the next chapter covers in detail, these commands can show you the layout, so you can decide where to go and how to get there. Once you can view and navigate the system, the following chapter introduces some ways of working with the actual files.

Dir

What it does: displays a list of files and folders inside a folder (directory)

Why use it: to list the contents of a folder, and optionally to filter or sort the results

How to use it:

Run 'dir'. You will see a list of folders and files in the current folder. The current folder is specified in the command prompt. The 'dir' command is short for directory, and running it shows you the contents of a directory.

Run 'explorer %cd%'. This will open Windows Explorer for the folder in the command prompt, the same folder as 'dir' just ran in. If you need a reference point to understand what 'dir' is doing, compare the command's output to the contents of the folders in Windows Explorer.

Now choose a folder from the list. You will see which items on the list are folders because they will have '<DIR>' displayed in the same row. Run 'dir' followed by the folder name, e.g. 'dir documents'. You will see a new list containing all the files and folders inside 'documents'.

This shows an important concept in how command line works, and not just for 'dir'. By default, commands are applied to the current directory, as displayed in the path of the command prompt. For example, depending on your system, your current folder may be something like 'C:\Users\YourNameHere'. Commands can be applied to other folders, or directory, paths if these are given as parameters. If you give an incomplete path, i.e. just a folder name, as a parameter, it is used relative to the current directory, i.e. inside of it. The command is then applied to 'C:\Users\YourNameHere\Documents'.

Maybe you want to look one folder further in. For example, if 'documents' contained a 'car' folder, you would run 'dir documents\car'. Try this out with a folder and subfolder on your system. You will see the contents. Directory names are separated by '\' characters (backslashes). Again, this works with commands in general, not just 'dir'.

You do not have to be limited by the current directory, however. If you give a complete path, one beginning with a drive, like 'C:', the command uses that instead, whichever folder you are currently in. In the example above, you might run 'dir C:\Users'. Choose a folder path from your system and run 'dir' followed by that path. You will see the contents of that folder, whatever you current directory is.

42

Most commands accept paths as parameters. If in doubt, just run their name plus '/?' to check their help information.

There are a lot of switches that can be used with 'dir'. They can do things like sort or filter the list of results. For example, run 'dir /o:s' to sort by file size, or 'dir /o:d' to sort by date. The main point here is that 'dir' shows directory contents.

Tree

What it does: displays the system of folders, subfolders, and files in the current directory

Why use it: to see what is in a folder before you navigate through it or change it

How to use it:

Run 'tree' to see the folders inside the current one, the folders inside those, and so on . If this command runs for a long time, hold down the 'control' key and press 'c' to cancel it. You can make the command run more quickly by choosing a folder with fewer subfolders, e.g. in the examples above for 'dir', the folder 'C:\Users\YourNameHere\Documents\Car' would have much less in it than, 'C:\Users'. Run 'tree' on a few folders until you find one of a manageable size.

The result of 'tree' is a kind of map of the folders on your system, showing which are inside which. Notice how each subfolder appears to branch off a 'parent' folder, while a parent folder may have many subfolder 'children'. It's like the way that tree branches split again and again towards their tips, but never join together. The folder system is a 'tree' structure.

Run 'tree /f' to include files in that map.

43

Navigation

Many commands affect, or display details of, locations in the file system: files, folders or drives. If you want to affect one of these locations, you could specify its name as a parameter of each command you use. However, if you have many commands which relate to the same folder, it would be easier to set that as the default.

You do this by navigating to the folder, making it the 'current directory'. The current directory, i.e. the folder you are in, is the default folder which commands use unless you specify otherwise. Commands operate on the contents of that location, e.g. listing the files it contains. Likewise, if you want to open a file, or run a batch script, in your current directory, you just type its name. If it is in another directory, you have to type the path too.

This chapter shows how to move around the file system. Once you know how to find folders, the next chapter shows some ways to work with any files inside of them.

Chdir (Cd)

What it does: gets or sets the current folder (directory)

Why use it: to move around the file system

How to use it:

Before starting to use 'cd', make some folders to navigate around in. Open the file system (Windows Explorer) and create a folder for all of your command line and batch scripting work. You could just call it 'batch'. In 'batch', create a folder called 'cd1' for all of your work on this command. Inside that folder, create two subfolders, 'folder1' and 'folder2'.

In Windows Explorer, you will see the series of folder names you are currently working within in the address bar at the top of the screen. Highlight (select) the whole text of the bar, e.g. 'C:\Users\Me\Documents\Batch\cd1', then right click and select 'copy' on the menu that appears. Open the command prompt. Type 'cd' followed by a space, then right-click inside the command window and select 'paste'. Press 'return' to run the command.

The command prompt will now show your new directory address, i.e. any commands you run will be run within that folder: 'cd1'. Run 'dir' to see the contents of your current folder. They should include 'folder1'.

Run 'cd folder1'. Notice how '\folder1' is now added to your command prompt. You just changed directory again, going into 'folder1' in 'cd1'.

Run 'cd' and you will see your current directory path displayed. It is the one you just moved into, the same one as displayed in the command prompt. Used without parameters, 'cd' just displays which folder you are in at the time.

Run 'cd..'. Notice how '\folder1' is now removed from your command prompt. You just moved into the parent folder of the one you were in.

Run 'cd\'. Notice how the command prompt only shows the drive letter, e.g. 'C:\>'.

So 'cd' lets you move around the file system by specifying either a complete directory path or a subfolder of the folder you are in, and it also supports moves upwards, to the parent folder or drive.

Having covered 'cd', this is a good time to explore some shortcuts available in the command window.

Press the 'up' key. This will bring your last command back to the prompt. Press 'up' until you get your original command, to go to 'cd1', and run that again.

Type 'cd f' then press the 'tab' key. You will see 'folder1' filled in for you, press 'tab' again for 'folder2'. Press 'enter' to go there.

If you use 'dir', or 'tree', to check the existing folders and 'cd' to move through them, you can navigate to anywhere in the drive. You can even 'look up' into parent folders by running 'dir..'. The use of '..' to represent the parent directory is not restricted to the 'cd' command. Run it and see.

Now run 'dir\'. You will see the contents of the drive. The use of '\' is also not restricted.

There is one more character with a special meaning, like the examples above. It is the '.' character, which represents the current directory itself. The current directory is already used by default though, so '.' is not needed in these examples.

Exercise – go to your batch folder (custom2.bat)

Write a batch script to change directory to your 'batch' folder. So that you can call it from the default command prompt, store the batch file in the folder matching that prompt. Open a new command window and run the file from that to test it. You can now use this script to go directly to your batch folder whenever you try out ideas from this course.

Reading, writing and redirecting text

Now that you can find files on the system, there is a lot you can do with them.

You can display (read) a file's text to the command line. After that, you might want to add (append) text to files, or replace (overwrite) their text entirely. You might want to make a new file, or copy an existing one.

This chapter covers all of that and more.

Test folders

From this point on, many commands act on files or folders, so you will need to make dummy files or folders to practise on. Each time you start work on a new command, create a new folder and name it after the command, e.g. 'type1'. Use 'cd' to go to that folder before you start running the new command.

Having a new folder for each command provides an environment to test it out in, without it affecting your other work. Putting the command name in the folder helps you find it again. Putting '1' on the end of the folder name helps you, and the computer system, know when you are running the command and when you are just referring to its folder.

If you have to create folders inside a command's main folder, call them 'folder1', 'folder2', etc. If you create files, call them 'file1', 'file2', and so on, and assume they will be text files. The examples, and any exercise answers, will use this naming system, except where stated otherwise.

Type

What it does: displays the whole contents of a file

Why use it: To access the contents of a file, either to display or to use them.

How to use it:

In your 'type1' folder, create a text file. In it, enter a few lines of text (the lines only need to be a few characters long each), copy and paste them down the file until you have made a block of text too big to fit on your screen.

Run 'type file1.txt'. You will see the whole contents of the file in the command window, although you may have to scroll up to read them from the beginning.

If you want to read through the contents of a file, or command output, a bit at a time, instead of displaying them all and then having to scroll back, you can use the 'more' command, which is covered in detail in book two. It is useful for large files.

Echo

What it does: Write lines of text to the command line or a file, or as input to other commands.

Why use it: To provide information to the user or another program, or to make / modify files for records or logs.

How to use it:

The command

Run 'echo Hello world!'. You will see the words repeated on the line below, followed by a new, blank, line. Echo writes characters to the current line and then starts a new line underneath.

Run 'echo.'. That is how to send a blank line using echo. You will see two blank lines below the command, as the command line displays an extra one by default. If you want to send an actual '.' character, put a space before it, after 'echo'.

The 'echo' command itself is simple. Because of this, it provides an easy way to test out some other features of the command line, as shown below.

Following up

Run 'echo Hello& echo world!'. You will now see one word above the other. The '&' sign (ampersand) makes the second command run immediately after the first, and works for commands in general, not just 'echo'. Run 'echo some text& dir' to see this in action.

Note that in the examples above, there is no space between the first command and the '&' character. This is because commands which process text strings, like 'echo', would include that space in the string. A lot of the time this doesn't matter: the user is unlikely to notice an extra space in the command window. However, if you were setting the value of a variable, as is covered later in this book, it could end up with an extra space in, which could stop it working properly.

You can run two commands from one line with '&', but you may also want a bit more control than '&' gives you. You may only want to run the second command if the first one works. For example, if you wanted to change to another directory and display its contents, you could run 'cd NotAFolder& dir'. If 'cd' could not find the folder, it would do nothing. Then 'dir' would run. This would display your original folder's contents, which would be confusing. Try running the command and see.

In a case like this, you need '&&'. That way you run the second command only if the first one completes without error. Run 'cd NotAFolder&& dir' and you will see only the error message from 'cd'.

Finally, you may wish to run a command only if the command before it does return an error, using '||'. For example, if you wanted to make it very obvious when a command failed, you could run 'cd NotAFolder|| color C1'. Try it out.

Exercise – two new lines (twoLines.bat)
How would you send two blank lines to the command window? If done correctly, this will make three blank lines appear below the prompt. You can do this from the command line directly or make a batch file to do it. Have a go.

Escape characters
In the examples above, using '&' ends the 'echo' command. This raises the question of how to display an '&' as text. The answer is to put a '^' (caret) before it in the command, which tells the computer to treat the ampersand as normal text (the caret 'escapes' the ampersand). The computer also drops the caret from the text it outputs. The caret is the main escape character for command line and batch scripting. If you want to send an actual '&' character, put a caret before it. Run 'echo some text ^& dir' to see how this works.

There are more characters like '&', that the system takes as being code unless you escape them. They include '^' itself. You may now be wondering how to display '^' as text. The answer is simple: '^^'. Run 'echo ^^' to see.

Redirection operators
The 'echo' command is central to batch scripting. It not only sends information to the command window, for the programmer or user to see, it also sends text as input to files, for saving, and to commands and programs for processing, or even to control those programs. To use it effectively, read on to learn about using 'echo' with redirection operators.

Run 'echo hello world>>file1.txt'. Run it again. If you check in your folder on Windows Explorer, file1 should now exist. If you open it, you will see your text on the first and second lines.

The '>>' operator adds text to the end of files (appends the text to them). If the file does not exist at the time of appending, the system creates a new file, gives it the name you specified, and writes in the text. So you just created a new file, wrote in some text (and started a new line), and wrote the same text onto the end, i.e. on the new line.

Now run 'echo hello world>file1.txt'. Open the file and you will see one line only.

The '>' operator sets the text in files (overwrites them). While useful in some cases, it also provides a very fast way to lose data, if care is not taken.

If the file does not exist, '>' creates a new file, just like '>>'.

This gives you an easy way to create a new batch file. Just go to the directory you want to keep it in, and run 'echo.>anyFileName.bat'. Of course, if you run 'notepad anyFileName.bat' you can do that, and/or open the file too. Try out both ways.

The redirection operators are not restricted to 'echo'. Run 'ipconfig>file1.txt'. Open the file again and you will see a copy of the command's output stored there.

Exercise – clear a file (clearFile.bat)
How would you clear a file, i.e. overwrite it with nothing, or at least, something very similar to nothing? Have a go: clear 'file1.txt'.

Exercise – redirect information (sysInfo.bat)
Use the command line to send the output of 'systeminfo' to its own text file. This is useful if you ever want to save any of the output. Once it is saved, it can also be opened and pasted into other programs.

Exercise – collect information (gather.bat)
Send 'ver', 'vol' and 'hostname' to the same file, to be stored together.

More on redirection
There is also a '<' operator, which allows commands to read from files. It works in a different way to the 'type' command. It is covered later in this book.

Some commands, such as 'copy' or 'timeout', perform actions, rather than providing information. However, they often still have output, such as counts of files copied or time passed, which appears on the command line. If you don't want to see this, you can use redirection. When you used redirection earlier, you may have noticed that text sent to files does not appear in the command window. You can also re-direct text to 'nul', which is like deleting it, and also stops it appearing to the user. This is demonstrated in the section on the 'timeout' command.

As with '&', the redirection operators are escaped with '^'. They too can be used with other commands. The 'echo' command is just one example.

The pipe operator
Another useful thing that 'echo' can do is send (pipe) input to other commands. The following examples should show how.

Run 'PAUSE' and then follow the instruction which the command prompt gives you.

The PAUSE command stops the command window and waits for the user to confirm that the computer should continue. This is particularly useful in batch scripts where information is displayed in the command window and the user needs time to read it before the script shuts itself down.

Many other commands also have prompts, usually requiring the user to make a decision and to type 'y' or 'n' for yes or no. Sometimes they ask for 'f' or 'd', for file or directory, and so on. How the user answers affects what the command does.

This creates a problem with using such commands in batch scripts, because if the user has to keep answering prompts, then the script keeps stopping. This delays the whole process and the user has to do more work, which is what batch scripts are created to overcome in the first place. The pipe operator '|', provides a way to work around this.

Run 'echo y| PAUSE'. The same prompt appears and is then skipped through. By piping 'y' to the PAUSE command, you answered the prompt as soon as it appeared, so the command was completed. The computer took the 'y' for user input.

Whilst you probably wouldn't pipe input to 'PAUSE', you can use 'echo' and '|' (pipe) to answer other prompts this way, sending the appropriate letter: a technique which can be used in some of the commands covered later.

You can also pipe text or command output to other commands. For example, if you wanted to sort the output of a command into alphabetical order, you would pipe it to the sort command. Run 'ipconfig| sort' to see an example of this. There is more on the topic of sorting in the next book.

Note that as with '&', '&&', '| |' and the redirection operators, it is a good idea to not put a space between your command and the pipe operator.

Turning echo on and off

Run 'echo'. You will see a message that 'ECHO is on'. What this means is that, when you run a batch script, commands will display in the command window. To see this, create a file called 'switch.bat'. In it, type 'ECHO some text'. Run the file from command line, i.e. type 'switch' and press enter. You will see that both the command to display a message, 'ECHO some text', and the message itself, 'some text', appear. If you just want to tell the user something, this is a very untidy way to do so.

So you need to run 'echo off'. Add this in at the start of your batch file, then add the lines 'ECHO more text' and 'ECHO even more' at the end, so that you have a four-line script. Now run it and see the result. You will see that after the 'echo off' line, the three messages are displayed neatly, one after the other, with no commands in between. They are more readable and user-friendly.

If you do need to display commands again, run 'echo on', and if you need to know whether they will display or not, just run 'echo'.

How can you switch 'echo' off for the 'echo off' command? You can use '@'. Put it at the start of a line to switch off 'echo' for that line only. You will see many batch files that start with the line '@echo off'.

Handles

The command line is text-based. The text falls into three main categories. There is input (standard input, or 'stdin'), usually from the user and their keyboard. There is output (stdout), such as when 'dir' returns a list of files. There is error text (stderr), such as the message you get if you run 'notACommand'. These sources of text are known as 'streams'. They are referred to in command line by the numbers 0, 1 and 2, respectively. These are known as their handles.

You can control these streams using their handles. For example, normally, if you run a command e.g. 'type notAFile.txt >>errorlog.txt', you send a blank output to the file and an error message to the command window which tells you that the file can't be found. However, run 'type notAFile.txt 2>>errorlog.txt', and you change everything. The command runs, and the error is sent to the log file. Open the file and take a look. You now have a way of logging any error generated by you commands, or in your batch scripts. Log files can be used to record which processes have been run, when, who by, what went right or wrong, and so on.

If you want to record both the output and the error to one file, you can do that too. Run 'type notAFile.txt >>log.txt 2>&1'. The ending '2>&1' re-directs 1 and 2, 'stdout' and 'stderr'. They both go to the file specified after '>>'. Now run 'echo text>>log.txt 2>&1'. The same ending does the same thing, whether the command produces output or error, it gets logged.

The '<' character re-directs to 'stdin'. It can be used to read text from files into commands. This is covered later in this book, in the section on the 'if' command.

Using parameters in your batch scripts

Create a batch file called 'params.bat'. In it, type:

    @echo off

    ECHO Parameter 1: %1

    ECHO Parameter 2: %2

    PAUSE

Now run 'params quiet mode'. You will see each word after the script name has been used as a parameter. Your script can use parameters, just like built-in commands do. To refer to a parameter value when designing a script, just put '%' then the number of its place after the script name, i.e. '%1' is 'quiet'.

If you want your parameters to have spaces in, enclose them in double quotes, like this: "not quiet". Run 'params "not quiet" mode'. You will see that the first two words appear in the place of

'%1'. They appear with the quotes still around them. To use the value without the quotes, change the parameters in your batch script to '%~1' and '%~2'. Run the script again. You will see that it uses the parameter values without the quotes.

In this example, the script just displays the parameters you give it. In the exercise below, the parameters you enter actually control what the script does.

Exercise – back up a file (backup.bat)

If you can read a file's text, make a new file and add the same text to it, you can effectively copy files, or rather, their contents. Make two text files 'file1.txt' and 'file2.txt'. Make a batch script to copy a file, like 'file1.txt', into a backup file. The backup should have the same name, but a backup extension, i.e. 'file1.bak'. Open the new file with notepad (or run 'type file1.bak') to see if the process worked.

When you can do this, change the script so it takes the file name as a parameter. Test the script works by backing up each file.

Other actions

The commands and operators in the last chapter can do a lot, especially when combined with other commands to make batch scripts.

The chapter after this one will show some core components of batch scripting, and start putting them to use. First though, this chapter will cover some other built-in commands worth knowing about.

Chkdsk

What it does: checks a disk for errors and/or repairs them

Why use it: to check the status of the hard disk. The command reports on errors on the disk, and/or fixes them. This can improve disk performance, e.g. it can make a computer run faster.

How to use it:

Note: This command makes changes to the computer hard disk, which stores its data. To ensure your data is protected while running it, make a copy of the disk contents first.

If this command is run without switches, it checks your hard disk for errors. If run with the '/f' switch it fixes them. Both ways can take a while to run.

There aren't any exercises on 'chkdsk' here. It's the kind of command that gets run occasionally, as part of maintaining a computer system. It's more of a utility than a regular command. It is widely used, so it's worth at least a mention here, and it can do more than this brief section covers. If you have a particular interest in disk management, you can run 'chkdsk /?' to see what else it can do. Otherwise, here's a brief walk-through (which is much quicker than running it to see what happens).

Typically, running 'chkdsk' finds errors on the disk and advises the user to run 'chkdsk /f' to fix them. Running that then prompts the user to confirm they want the fix to continue next time the computer starts up. This, of course, means that the computer has to be restarted to finish the job, which leads on to the next command.

Shutdown

What it does: shuts down or restarts a computer, or logs off a user.

Why use it: many reasons, including restarting a machine after an installation, so that the machine immediately operates with the new setup

How to use it:

Have you ever installed an update on your PC and seen the system tell you it needs to restart before the update takes effect? If so, you already know a major use of the 'shutdown' command. This command also has a parameter to specify which computer to shutdown, i.e. the IP address of a connected machine on a network, so you can use it to shutdown or restart computers other than your own. This makes it much more useful, especially in IT support, which so often involves turning machines off and on, as at least part of troubleshooting them.

Also, this command allows you to stop a computer shutting down. You do this with the '/a', for 'Abort', switch. You may have to be fast, to use it in time, though.

As with 'chkdsk', there are no exercises for this command, as restarting a computer repeatedly would get tedious very quickly. Run 'shutdown /?', or just 'shutdown', to see the help for this command. Take special note of the R, F, T, and M switches. The 'R' switch (written '/r') makes the system restart. The 'F' switch makes it shut down and restart 'forcefully', i.e. the computer does not refuse to shut down because it has other programs running. The 'T' switch and its time parameter allow you to set a delay for the shutdown, or specify no delay, i.e. '/t 000'. Finally the 'M' switch, followed by two backslashes and an IP address, e.g. '/m \\10.20.30.40', allows you to shutdown another computer on the network.

There are other switches, as detailed in the help, for logging off, shutting down without restarting, etc.

Performing a restart is a common task. However, once you have restarted a computer, you will want to use it again, at least to check it is working as you expect. With a local machine, i.e. the one you are on, this is no problem. With a remote machine on your network, which may span countries, it is. One way to test if a computer is on is to try to connect to it. This leads on to the next command.

Ping

What it does: tests the connection speed between your system and another

Why use it: to check a device is connected to your network and/or is switched on

How to use it:

You can ping an IP address, hostname, or even a website address. For example, if you run 'ping www.(website name here).com', you get a report of the connection speed, in milliseconds, between your computer and your chosen website. Your computer sends a signal to the website's IP address, waits for a response, and reports the time it took, or that it got no response.

Run 'hostname' and then ping the name it displays. As you are connecting to your own computer, this should be a very fast connection. You will also see the IP address for the hostname displayed. If not, run 'ping /4 YourHostName'. This will give you the IP address in its familiar format.

So, if you know the hostname of a remote computer, you can ping it to find which IP address the hostname converts to. Hostnames are often easier to remember than an IP address of up to twelve digits. They are often customised, and named systematically. This may be as simple as company PC number five having the hostname 'PC5'.

Equally, you may only know the IP address. The IP addresses on a network may be numbered systematically, e.g. PC5 might end in '.5' and PC6 in '.6'. This can even be easier to work with in some cases. You can also ping IP addresses directly.

If you run 'ping' with the '-t' switch, you get a continuous report. This is useful when monitoring a remote computer. For example, if the computer stops responding, then starts again, you know that it was disconnected then reconnected, at least in some way. It could mean the computer has been restarted, or that its network cable was unplugged temporarily. Note that a computer does not have to load up fully to respond to a ping. A response only indicates that the computer has got far enough through the start-up process to be able to communicate with the network.

The 'ping' command is a networking fundamental, and can do a lot more than the above. However, while this course covers working across networks, to cover networking itself would take a whole new course entirely. So having introduced 'ping', it's time to move on.

Timeout

What it does: Makes the command wait for a specified length of time

Why use it: To make a program execute after another has started or run, to give the user time to note something, or to execute commands at intervals

How to use it:

Run 'timeout /t 5' to see what this does. Run 'timeout /t 5 >nul' to see it countdown silently, i.e. without displaying the countdown on screen.

This command can make a program stop and wait. Sometimes, that can be a very useful thing. Some of the batch scripts later on will show why.

Runas

What it does: runs programs with the permissions of another user, i.e. not the one logged in, e.g. when connected to a remote computer which someone else is logged in to.

Why use it: to open, on a user account, programs which are otherwise restricted.

How to use it:

In many organisations, the systems are set up to prevent users running certain programs, often for the security of the system. However, an IT technician working on a user's machine may need to open such programs, e.g. task manager, while the user is still logged in. This command would allow the technician to run a specified program, with their own access permissions, and do so from within the user's account. It's worth being aware of, in case you ever need to do this.

Variables

The last two chapters begin to show some of the potential of the command line. But commands can do a lot more than that. One of the biggest advantages of using command line is the potential for automation.

Useful sequences of commands can be recorded in a batch file. The contents of this file are known as a batch script. A user can run the batch file, and therefore the scripted commands, as if they are a single action. The script handles the details.

A good comparison would be speed-dial, where you select someone's name on your mobile, and the machine enters all the digits of their phone number for you. It follows the sequence you saved.

However, if the tasks are not always exactly the same, a simple command sequence may fail. In phone systems, if your contact changes their number, your speed-dial stops working. In computer systems, for example, the user may target different files each time, or be unsure whether the target files exist at all.

This chapter, and the next, show ways to make batch scripts more flexible, to cope with change and uncertainty. This chapter shows how to get values from the user or the computer, values which may change between or during the times the script is run. The next chapter shows how to make scripts that run commands only under certain conditions, i.e. scripts that react to their environment.

Set
What it does: Assigns values to variables and displays environmental variables

Why use it: To store inputs, whose values may be unknown when the program is run, providing a flexible way to work with those values

How to use it:

The command
Run 'set'. You will see a list of information, each new line containing text, an '=' sign, and then more text. For example, in the list, you will see 'OS' for 'operating system' and that it 'equals' a version of Windows, e.g. 'Windows_NT'. You may also see values for your username, computer name, and so on. These are the 'environmental' variables: running 'set' displays them for you. Variables are effectively names that refer to information. They are useful because scripts can refer to the same variable name, even if the value it holds changes.

Run 'echo %os%' to display just the contents of that variable. Substitute 'os' for any other variable name to display their contents instead. For example, run 'echo %systemdrive%'. You will see from these examples that the case of the variables does not affect the how command runs: %os% is the same as '%OS%'.

You may have noticed, when running 'set', that some variable names are given all in uppercase, and others not. There are conventions regarding how to capitalise variable names, but this book will ignore them and just use camel case, like 'myVariableName', with initial letters capitalised from the second word onwards. This is to make all the variable names easier to read and understand.

There are also a few variables which 'set' does not list. Run 'echo %time%', for example, or 'echo %date%'. More of these will be introduced later in the course.

63

From the above examples, it is clear that variables can be accessed without 'set'. However, as the command's name suggests, you do need it to modify variables (set their values), or to create new ones. Variables are essential to writing flexible batch files.

Run 'set string=hello world'. Run 'echo %string%'. You have just created, and used, a variable. As with the built-in environmental variables above, the new variable's value is displayed.

Naming your variables

If you use 'set' to create a new variable, make sure that a variable with the same name does not already exist. You can do this by running 'set' and reading through the A-Z variable list it displays.

If you set the value of an existing (i.e. environmental) variable, you may affect the way your command window works. For example, run 'set prompt=hello', to see an example of this effect. Run 'prompt' or re-open the command window to reverse this change. While this example wouldn't affect much, setting other environmental variables can change the way your subsequent commands work, or stop them working. So it's good to check your variable name is unique first.

Accepting user input

Run 'set /p string=enter text: '. Then type some words on the next line, press return, and echo the string as before. You will see your words displayed. P is for prompt. When you ran the command, it prompted the user, in this case you, to enter what the content of the variable should be. This is useful in batch files where the user might want to set the variable to a different value each time they run your script.

The prompt switch allows users to input variables into the script part-way through. This gives an alternative to entering all the variables as parameters at the beginning.

Exercise – log user input (logIn.bat)

Make a batch script to accept text from a user and automatically log it to a new line of a text file. Then modify the script to include in each record the date, time and user who logged it. You can use 'set' to find variables that will help you do this.

Exercise – log command output (logOut.bat)

Make a batch script to accept and run commands from a user and automatically log the output to a new line of a text file, not the command window.

Exercise – log errors (logErr.bat)

Make a batch script to accept and run commands from a user and automatically log any errors they produce to a new line of a text file, not the command window.

Processing numbers

Variables are treated as strings by default, even if the string is '123' treats it as just a list of digits, the way you think of your phone number. This is natural in the text-based command line environment, but variables can also hold numbers that need to be used as numbers. To make 'set' treat variables that way, we can use the '/a' switch. A is for 'Arithmetic'.

Run 'set /a mynumber=1+2' then 'echo %mynumber%'. You should get '3'.

Run 'set number1=2' and 'set number2=4'. Adding the variables should give six. Run 'set number3=number1+number2' then 'echo %number3%'. It doesn't work. The command will not do sums without the A switch. You just get '2+4'. To set the third number correctly, you need to run 'set /a number3=number1+number2'.

As long as you use the A switch each time, i.e. on each line, using numbers is straightforward. Replace the '+' with '-' for subtraction, '*' for multiplication, of '/' for division. These symbols are known as operators, e.g. '/' is the division operator. There is also a '%' operator, the modulus operator, which calculates the modulus or remainder of a division. For example, '7%2' is one, because two goes into seven three times, leaving one left over.

Numbers and networks

The modulus operator is useful in cases such as dealing with IP addresses. These are the numeric internet/network addresses with formats like '192.168.10.7'. IP addresses are effectively assigned in groups of two-hundred-and-fifty-six, as each of the four numbers that make them up has a range from 0 to 255. They are often assigned sequentially e.g. computer number seven has a '7' in the IP address, while computer fifty has a '50' in the same place. When hundreds of IP addresses are in use, computer number 256 exceeds the capacity of this system, and, to maintain the logic, the network engineers assign two of the four IP numbers to specifying which computer is which. The IP now contains not only '0.1' to '0.255', but also '1.0' which may continue to '1.255' then '2.0' and so on.

The second number, in each of the above pairs, is the remainder of the computer number divided by 256. The first number is the computer number divided by 256, and rounded down, which the command line does anyway. So now you can calculate the parts of the IP address, and just need to know how to combine them. After working with text is explained later on, there is an exercise on making IP addresses. Calculating IP addresses is useful for working over networks.

Shorthand number processing

Like many scripting and programming languages, batch script has a more compact way to specify changes you want to make to variables. Where you could add '3' to 'mynumber' by running 'set /a myNumber=myNumber+3', you can shorten this to 'set /a myNumber+=3'. This works for all the operators, not just '+'.

Exercise - find the remainder (mod.bat)

Make a batch script to find the remainder of one number divided by a second. It should take both the numbers as parameters

Exercise – division (divideA.bat)

Make a batch script to actually divide one number by a second. It also should take these numbers as parameters

Exercise – square a number (square.bat)

Make a batch script to multiply a number by itself.

Processing strings

The command line is text-based. Text is made up of sequences of characters. Any sequence of characters is known as a string. These strings can be used, or changed, and that means targeting and working with smaller sections of them. These are known as substrings, but they are still also strings, just like subfolders are also folders. Read on to learn how to find a substring; from the left, right, or middle of a string; and to replace or remove a substring.

Processing substrings by position

Below are some examples of using strings, followed by the rules describing how they work.

Before starting, run 'set string=hello world!', so that you have a string to experiment on.

Example: Run echo %string:~3%. You should see 'lo world!', all but the first three characters. Run echo %string:~-3%. You should see 'ld!' the last three characters.

Rule: use %string:~n% to take the right-hand part of a string, where 'n' is the start position, or 'offset', measured in number of characters. Positive values of 'n' are counted from the left, i.e. the start, of the string, with the first character having an offset of zero (because there is nothing between it and the start of the file), the second having an offset of one, and so on. That's why, in the example above, an offset of three gives you the fourth character onwards.

Negative values of 'n' are counted from the right, i.e. the end, of the string. The characters to the right of 'n' are then read.

The examples here use 'echo' so that you can try things out without needing to reset 'string' each time. But you can set string values in the same way that 'echo' displays them. If you wanted to keep the value of a substring, you could, for example, run 'set substring=%string:~3%', then run 'echo %substring%' to check it worked. If you wanted to change the value of 'string' cutting it down to only a substring of itself, you could run 'set string=%string:~3%'. If you try these out, reset 'string' to 'hello world!' at the end.

Example: run echo %string:~3,4%. You should see 'lo w', the first four characters, which includes the space, after the offset: '3'. Run echo %string:~3,-4%. You should now see 'lo wo', the characters after the start position '3', up to the end position '-4' (four characters from the end of the string).

Rule: use %string:~n,m% to take the middle part of a string, where 'm' is the end position. Positive values of m are read as a length from the left (after 'n'), i.e. included. Negative values of 'm' are counted from the right and read up to, i.e. excluded.

To take the left-hand part of a string, use the above method, but set 'n' to zero.

To be precise, if 'n' and 'm' are positive, 'n' is the start position, relative to the left end of the string and 'm' is the end position relative to that 'n'. If either 'n' or 'm' is negative, its position is instead relative to the end of the string. This can be a little hard to remember from reading, but it is easy to practise.

Processing substrings by content
Strings can also be processed by the text they contain.

Example: run 'echo %string:hello=hi%'. You should see that 'hi' has replaced 'hello' in the string. Run 'echo %string:hello=%'. You should see that hello has been removed from the string, i.e. it has been replaced, but by nothing.

Rule: use string %string:substring=x% to replace/remove part of a string where x is the replacement text, even if that replacement is an empty string.

To join strings together (or 'concatenate' them), simply put them next to each other. For example, run 'echo %string% and some more text'.

To split strings into sections, e.g. to get each value of a CSV file, you can use a 'for' loop. These are covered in book three.

Stored commands
The command line expands variables into strings. The command line runs strings as commands. Taken together, this means that the command line can run commands from variables.

To see this, run 'set col=color 50'. Then run '%col%'.

This effect is worth noting. You could use it to shorten your code, for example if you have one command you run many times in a script. An obvious example would be something like 'ECHO.'. You could store it in, and replace it with, '%e%'.

However, storing commands in variables blurs the line between data and commands. You may prefer to avoid this. Keep in mind, though, that the command window will try to run any string that makes it to the command prompt. You can end up running commands you thought were data by accident!

Exercises

There are a lot of exercises here. This is partly because there is a lot to practise with strings. It is also because, with 'set', you can finally create some more advanced batch scripts. This allows you to make scripts that use and combine the commands covered earlier.

Exercise – make an IP address (getIP.bat)

Make a script to take a number and output an IP address, as discussed earlier. Assume that the IP address always starts with '1.2.' and that the last two numbers are generated from the input.

Exercise – left (left10.bat)

Make a script to take a string input, and return the first ten characters from it. The number of characters to return will have to be fixed in the script for now, but this can be made a variable for the user to set as well. That would be better left until after the concept of delayed expansion is covered though, which is in book two.

Exercise – right (right10.bat)

Make a script to take a string input, and return the last ten characters from it.

Exercise – middle (char3.bat)

Make a script to take a string input, and return the third character from it.

Exercise – replace (trim.bat)

Make a script to take a string input, and return the string with any double spaces cut down to single spaces.

Exercise – Americanise (UKtoUS.bat)

Make a script to replace some common words in a single-line text file with their equivalent in another dialect of English, or another language if you prefer. Make sure to replace at least two different words in the same file. Once the 'for' command is covered, in book three, this script can be changed to convert multi-line text files too. Single-line files do exist, though: removing the line breaks from a file is one way to compress it.

Goto

The 'goto' command comes later in the course, but the following script shows a bit of what it can do. Create a batch file called 'loop.bat' and in it type:

    @ECHO OFF

    ECHO Here is some text

    :startLoop

        ECHO and here is some more

        PAUSE

    GOTO startLoop

Run the script. It repeats the commands after ':startLoop' endlessly, assuming you keep pressing a key at each pause. Use 'ctrl + c' or close the command window to stop it.

You will need to run some commands in a loop to complete the next exercise. The 'goto' command lets you do that. It sends the command line back to a label like ':startLoop'. You make a line a label by starting it with a colon ':'.

Exercise – messenger (writer.bat, reader.bat, flush.bat)

Make a batch file called 'writer.bat' to prompt the user to enter a message, then loop back and prompt again when they do. Have it add each message to the end of a text file, along with the name of who sent it. Make another batch file caller 'reader.bat'. Customise it so that when it opens, its command window looks different to 'writer'. Make 'reader' display the contents of the text file, and update itself every few seconds. Open both windows and use them to have a conversation. If you are on a network, it can even be a two-sided, or multi-sided, conversation, rather than a one-person forum. Finally, make a batch script to delete the contents of your text file when you are done, call it 'flush.bat'.

Exercise – security (writer2.bat)

Send the message 'gotcha & dir' through the writer window. Notice how the output of 'dir' is displayed in the reader window. This means that the reader actually ran the command that the writer wrote, just by having 'reader.bat' open. This is a security flaw for the reader: imagine if the writer had sent through commands to shutdown the machine, delete files, or worse. In your code, escape any '&' characters the user may input, so this can't happen again. Make sure to test it.

There are other ways to bypass this 'security measure', of course, but this program does shed light on how command line works.

Decisions

Variables represent changeable, often unpredictable or unknown, values in a script. They let the script 'see' some of its environment. By responding to the value of a variable, the script can respond to its environment.

This chapter shows how to control those decisions and responses.

If

What it does: runs code when specified conditions are met.

Why use it: to write programs that can cope with a variety of situations, and are therefore more reliable

How to use it:

Using 'if' with 'else', 'not', and 'exist'

Create a file with the text '<!DOCTYPE html>' as the first line. Save it with an '.html' extension (you can set the extension in the 'save as' dialog box in Notepad). Copy the file. Modify the copy, so it has different text in the first line. Call them 'file1.html' and 'file2.html', i.e. follow the usual naming system.

Create a batch file 'isInFolder.bat' and in it type:

```
@ECHO OFF

IF EXIST %1 (ECHO File found) ELSE ECHO File not found
```

Run the script from the command line using 'isInFolder file1.html'. Run 'isInFolder notAFile.txt'. The 'EXIST %1' part of the command takes the filename you entered and outputs a true or false value back to 'IF' based on whether it found the file in the current folder. When it gets a 'true' value, the if-clause runs the command before 'else'. When it gets a false value, it runs the command after 'else'. If you prefer to break up the if-clause, for readability, you can format it as follows:

> @ECHO OFF
>
> IF EXIST %1 (
>
> > ECHO File found
>
>) ELSE (
>
> > ECHO File not found
>
>)

Using the method above, you can also run multiple commands in each case. To see this, add the line 'ECHO in this folder' to the script above, directly below each of the other two 'ECHO' commands. Then run the script again with the same file name parameters as before.

Note that the placement of both '(' and ')' is critical to any multi-line statement. Unless a line ends inside one of these pairs, the line following it is run as an independent command, i.e. outside the if-clause.

You can use 'if' to check other things too, writing the statement the same way: IF condition-to-test (action-if-true) ELSE action-if-false.

The way a command, or script, is written is known as its syntax.

The 'ELSE' part is optional, so if the action you want to take in 'false' cases is to do nothing, leave 'else' out. In those cases, with the single-line 'if', you could also leave the '()' out, as they are only there to mark the separation between the true and false actions.

If you only want your script to act in 'false' cases, you can reverse the condition of the test by putting 'NOT' before it, i.e. 'IF NOT…'

Then you can replace the old action-if-true and still drop the 'else' clause.

Comparing strings

So what else can you do with 'if'? You can compare strings. Strings are everywhere. You just created two html files with strings in. The next script uses 'if' to check the first line of a file, to see if it matches the standard text used in HTML5 documents: '<!DOCTYPE html>'. It then reports if the file is a HTML5 document.

Create a batch file 'isHTML5.bat' and in it type:

    @ECHO OFF

    SET /P Line1=<%1

    IF "%Line1%"=="<!DOCTYPE html>" (SET Result=html5) ELSE SET Result=not html5

    ECHO %Result%

Run 'isHTML5 file1.html' then 'isHTML5 file2.html'. The file extensions are the same, but your new html5 detector tells you which files are up-to-date with the latest version of html.

Note that it isn't always necessary to put the double-quotes around the string each side of '=='. It is necessary in this case because the strings can contain a space, which would normally indicate the end of a string. Adding the quotes gets around this, but they have to be added to both sides, to balance out.

A neat trick

The script above also uses redirection, with '<'. The '<' redirection operator reads the first line of text, from the html file, into the command, setting the variable. You may notice that 'set' in the script above uses the prompt switch '/p', for user input. Because '<'

redirects to the user input (stdin), the command works as if the user had typed in the text themselves.

The '<' redirection operator reads only the first line of text from the html file. That could be considered limiting, compared to, say, the 'more' or 'type' commands, but this script takes advantage of it. Alternative file-reading commands often read through file contents as a whole. This means they have to process all the text, which complicates the script and/or makes it run more slowly. By using '<' to take just the first line, the script above avoids the need to process any other lines of text. This makes it simpler to write and faster to run.

Case-sensitivity

Now, suppose your HTML documents aren't as standardised as this. Change the header of your html5 file to '<!doctype html>', all lower case. Now run your batch script again and see if the file is recognised as html5. It won't be. You need to switch off case-sensitivity. Fortunately, there is a switch for this: the '/i' switch.

Replace:

>   IF "%Line1%"=="<!DOCTYPE html>" (SET Result=html5) ELSE SET Result=not html5

With:

>   IF /I "%Line1%" EQU "<!DOCTYPE html>" (SET Result=html5) ELSE SET Result=not html5

The 'EQU' is a comparison operator for 'equals'. The '/i' switch makes the comparison case-insensitive so that capital and lowercase letters are viewed as equal. Run the script now and you will see it confirm that the file is html5, i.e. it ignored the different cases of the two strings.

Comparing numbers

With operators like 'EQU', you can also compare two numbers. The number comparison operators are: equal (EQU), not equal (NEQ), less than (LSS), greater than (GTR), less than or equal to (LEQ), and greater than or equal to (GEQ).

For example, if a script take months as a parameter, you could include a line to accept input values up to twelve, i.e.

    @ECHO OFF

    IF %1 LEQ 12 (ECHO Input accepted!) ELSE ECHO There are only 12 months! & EXIT /B

To try this out, create a 'month.bat' file. Enter the above line in it. Run it using 'month 1' then 'month 13'. The 'exit /b' command above tells the batch script to stop without running any more commands (if there were any), so it doesn't try to process the thirteenth month.

Making your script more reliable

Finally, you may wish to check whether a variable exists at all. The 'if' command's 'defined' keyword lets you do this. Run the line below in the command window:

    IF DEFINED cd (ECHO Variable is defined!) ELSE ECHO Variable is not defined!

Note that the variable name, 'cd', is used, rather than its value, '%cd%'. The variable is defined by its name, not its value, so this is what the command checks. To see the command work with an undefined variable, run it again and replace 'cd' with something else, e.g. 'cod'.

This kind of check is a useful form of data validation, ensuring that scripts have the correct information before they run other commands, and providing feedback to the user.

Handling errors

There is also an 'if' syntax specifically for use with the '%errorlevel%' variable. This is covered in the 'exit' command section of the course, where error levels are introduced.

Exercise – check a file exists (isHere.bat)

Write a batch script to check if a user-specified file exists.

Exercise – infinity (divideB.bat)

Change your division script to avoid divide by zero errors and return the answer 'infinity' instead.

Exercise – absolute (absA.bat, absB.bat)

Find the difference between two numbers, as an absolute value, i.e. a value without a plus or minus sign in front, no matter which order the numbers are typed after the script name. Write a script that corrects any negative values after subtracting. Write another version that always subtracts in the right order, so no correction is required.

Exercise – command selector (info.bat)

Make a batch script to prompt users to press options 1-3 to run 'ver', 'vol' or 'hostname' and return the output.

Exercise – validation (info2.bat)

Make a copy of the script and modify it so that it warns the user if they select an option that does not exist, i.e. '4' or 'some text'.

Volume 2

Introduction

Welcome to Learn Command Line and Batch Scripting Fast, Volume 2! This book is part two of a three part course for people who want to learn how to use command line, write batch scripts, or both. It follows on directly from the last book, building on the concepts already covered. It is designed to cover as much as possible, as concisely as possible, with plenty of examples and practice exercises. It uses the same naming system for any dummy files and folders used in the examples.

Naming System

The examples in this book name folders and files in a standard way, to simplify setting them up to practise on.

The system is simple. For each new command, create a folder to practice in. For example, for 'echo', create an 'echo1' folder. Then change directory to that folder in the command prompt. If you create any files inside it, make them text files and name them, 'file1', 'file2', etc, unless otherwise stated. If you create folders there, call them 'folder1', 'folder2', etc. If these folders have subfolders, use 'subfolder1', 'subfolder2', etc.

Organisation

The chapters of this book are written as part of a course, to be read sequentially. However, the book can be divided into three parts, each largely independent of the other, except for the exercises, which show how to integrate the concepts covered. The first part shows how to access and process file contents. The second shows commands central to controlling batch scripts. The third shows how to control the file system, including how to create, change, delete, and copy files and folders. This continues the progression from passively accessing data and systems to actively changing them.

Command syntax

The syntax, i.e. the switches and parameters, such as file paths, and the order of these, required to use each command is included in the command line help, accessed by typing the command name, followed by '/?'. As such, it is not repeated in this book, which focuses on examples you can try out yourself, explanations of how and why to use the commands, and exercises to practice them. When you do need to check syntax beyond what the examples show, the help provides a ready reference in your command console, so the information doesn't need to be duplicated here.

File Contents and Filtering

You can use command line to read file contents. You did so earlier, with 'type'. The 'type' command displays a file's whole text, for you to read.

But what if you don't want the whole text?

In that case, you need the commands in this chapter. They work with what's inside a file.

The commands are:

More: for showing the contents a bit at a time

Sort: for showing the contents in order, e.g. alphabetically

Find and Findstr: for showing lines that contain certain text, or patterns of text

FC: for displaying lines that don't match between two files

Comp: for displaying characters that don't match between two files

These commands also work on command output, such as the results of 'systeminfo' or 'ipconfig'. So if you want to display just the line containing your IP address, for example, you can do that, using 'find'. If you use 'find' in this way, it is known as a command line filter.

If you can display text in the command window, you can store it elsewhere, including in other files and batch script variables. By learning how to display the text you want, you are halfway to being able to re-use it elsewhere.

82

More

What it does: gets and displays one command window's worth of text

Why use it: to load and read text in manageable chunks

How to use it:

Note: If the command alone is typed, it makes everything you type into the command window appear a second time, whenever you press return. You then have to press 'ctrl + C', or close and re-open the command window, to make it work normally again.

Displaying command output: the basics
Run 'systeminfo' and wait for it to finish running. Have a brief look at the output in your command window, scrolling up as far as possible to read from the top. There is a lot of text. It will not fit on one screen. It may even not fit in the command window.

To manage large amounts of text like this, use the 'more' command.

Run 'systeminfo| more'. The pipe '|' operator passes the output of 'systeminfo' into the 'more' command. You should now see one screen of text and a 'more' prompt at the end. At that prompt, you can press space to display the next page, or press return for just the next line. Try this out now.

Displaying command output: extras
You can also display or skip a specified number of lines, display the contents of the next file (if you are using 'more' to read files, rather than command output) or quit reading part way through.

Run the same command, taking a note of the line where it stops, and type 'P'. A 'Lines' prompt will appear. Type a number and press return: the same number of new lines will appear. Then press space until you see a long list of numbered updates (they may be called 'hotfixes'). Now that you are partway through this list, note the last number on it, press 's' and then enter a number at the 'Lines' prompt. Read back and you will see from the 'hotfix' numbers that the command window has skipped over that many lines.

If you needed to get the line number i.e. how far you are through the file, press '=', to display it at the 'more' prompt.

When entering the 'more' command to start with, the switches give you a different set of options for formatting output. These include the '/c' switch for clearing the command prompt before printing to it. Try this out, for comparison to the 'CLS' command.

File reading basics
You can use 'more' to read through files too. To try this out, first make a suitably large file. An easy way to do this is to run 'systeminfo>sysinfo.txt' to redirect the output of that command into a text file. You can now run 'more sysinfo.txt' to read through the file.

Although 'systeminfo' outputs a lot of text for a command, files can contain far more. Displaying it a bit at a time can make it easier to read through.

If you wanted, you could even list several file names, with spaces between, and read them all through.

File reading extras
Open the file and add a few blank lines near the top. Run 'more /s sysinfo.txt'. You will see that the group of blank lines has been compressed into 1 blank line.

If you redirect this output to another file, i.e. 'more /s sysinfo.txt>sysinfo2.txt', you have a tool to strip any 'extra' blank lines out of files.

Finally, run 'more sysinfo.txt sysinfo2.txt'. You should see your first file, with its blank lines in the command window. Press 'f' at the prompt. You will then see the copy without the multiple blank lines. If you separate file names with spaces like this, you could read through multiple files this way. You can even avoid typing out a long list of file names, by using the wildcard character: '*'.

If you had, or made, a directory full of text files you needed to look inside, you could save a lot of typing by running 'more *.txt'. The wildcard would display all the folder's text files and allow you to quickly check the contents of each, just by pressing 'f' each time you finish checking a file. If you had say, twenty files to check through, this could save a lot of opening and closing in Notepad.

There are even more switches and options for using the 'more' command, instructions for which can be found by running 'more /?' in the command window.

Exercise – quickly reading through files (scanLogs.bat)

Suppose you have a whole folder full of log files, and you want to quickly be able to check through their contents. Can you make a script that would do this?

First set up a 'logs' folder. In it, create three text files. Name them 'log1.txt', 'log2.txt', and so on. Type in each 'this is log number (whatever the number is)'. Then enter or paste a few screens worth of filler text, e.g. from your 'sysinfo.txt' file, in after it.

Now create a batch script that lets you read through any and all 'log' files in one command window, pressing 'space' to see the next screen, and 'f' to see the next file. Make the script work no matter how many log files there may be.

Sort

What it does: puts file contents or command output into alphabetical order, line-by-line

85

Why use it: to make it easy to check a list for specific items

How to use it:

Sort: the basics
Note: If the command alone is typed, it prompts you to type more into the command window. You then have to press 'control + C' to stop this prompting and to make the open command window work normally again. When you do this the lines you type will reappear, sorted into alphabetical order.

Before using 'sort', you need data to use it with. It doesn't matter what the data is, so long as it is text in a file. You could use a list of fish if you like, so let's do that. Create a text file, 'fish.txt', with these words, one on each line: 'cod', 'barracuda', 'anchovy', 'eel', 'dogfish'.

Run 'sort fish.txt'. The fish will now be listed in the correct order, in command line. Their order in the text file is unaffected.

Run 'sort fish.txt /o myfish.txt'. The 'o' is for output file. Your output file is 'myfish.txt'. In this file, the fish will be sorted alphabetically.

Exercise – sort inside files (sortFile.bat)
Can you sort the fish in the first file without using any other files? Try this now. Make a script that runs from command line, and takes the file name as a parameter.

Exercise – the '/r' switch (sortFileR.bat)
In the same script, add the '/r' switch before the '/o' switch of 'sort'. Run it again. Done right, this will sort the file contents in reverse order.

Sort: from here on in
In one of the files, insert the letter 'a' followed by a space in front of each line. In the line with 'a cod', replace the 'a' with 'z'. You

would now expect the 'z cod' line to be at the end after a sort. Run 'sort /+3 fish.txt' and check if this happened.

It made the comparison start from character number three in each line. This allows you to skip characters which are irrelevant to the sort, like standard text at the start of each line. Also, some types of data file are composed of rows of multiple fixed length strings, each length forming part of a 'column'. By skipping a set number of characters in each row, you can sort by different column values.

Performance issues

In your fish file, press 'control + a' to select the contents, press 'end', and then press 'control + v' to paste them, doubling the amount of text and therefore the file size. Repeat this several times. Doubling the size ten times makes the file over a thousand times bigger. We need a big file to see the effect of the next command. If you right-click on the file and select properties, you should see the file size: 3-10kb should be big enough.

Delete the output file 'myfish.txt'.

Run 'echo started at %time% & sort fish.txt /o myfish.txt & echo stopped at %time%'.

You don't need to see the list of fish, but these commands will give you the times when the sort started and stopped. This allows you to see how fast the sort ran.

Delete the output file 'myfish.txt'.

Add the switch and parameter '/l C' to your command string. That is, run 'echo started at %time% & sort /l C fish.txt /o myfish.txt & echo stopped at %time%'.

Which of the two sorts was finished in less time?

You should find that the '/l C' sort was much faster. My sort completed in 40% less time. For this file size, on a local computer, it is still a small difference (milliseconds), but if you do need to make your sorts run faster, this does the job. This option uses the '/l', or 'locale', switch, with the 'C' locale, the only other locale available. It sorts characters by their binary codes, which is what speeds up the process.

You can also use 'sort' as a command output filter, in the same way as 'more'. To see an example, run 'ipconfig| sort'.

Find

What it does: Gets or counts lines containing specified text from files or command output.

Why use it: To check for specific values, or errors, within files, or to re-use lines containing them

How to use it:

Find: the basics

Create a file and write three lines of text in it. Make sure the middle line contains the word 'Target', with a capital 'T'. Copy and paste the lines down the file, then paste again, so you have nine lines in the file.

Run 'find "target" file1.txt'. This displays the name of your file, but nothing else. It hasn't found the target text because it was searching for 'Target' with a capital T. Changing the T in 'target' to uppercase would fix this, but suppose you want to find text regardless of upper and lower case.

Run 'find /i "target" file1.txt'. You should now see three lines under the file name. The '/i' switch makes the search case-insensitive, so it now succeeds. Where the target text is found, the command returns the whole line containing it.

Find: the other switches

Run 'find /i /n "target" file1.txt'. Now you will see the line numbers where your results were found. N is for 'number'.

Run 'find /i /c "target" file1.txt'. This displays only the total number of lines containing the target text. C is for 'count'. Note that it does not count the number of times the target text appears. If you put 'Target' on the same line twice, it gets counted once.

Run 'find /i /v "target" file1.txt'. You will see the all the lines not containing your target text.

Exercise – combining switches (mismatchTotal.bat)

Just for practice: can you display a count of the lines which don't contain the target text? Have a go. Keep 'target' as your target, and 'file1.txt' as your file, but make a batch script to take them as parameters. Try a few ideas out in the command line first, if it helps.

Find: extras

Find can also search multiple files, if you separate their names with spaces, or take command output from a pipe '|'.

To pipe text to the command, follow the format in the example below.

Run 'systeminfo| find "OS"'. This command will find and display the lines of your computer's system information which refer to its OS, or Operating System, e.g. Microsoft Windows 8.1. It might also catch a few similar bits of text, like 'BIOS', but it is still a useful tool for filtering large blocks of text like this.

Exercise – searching command output (bootTime.bat)

Can you alter the command above to find out when the computer was last turned on, i.e. the 'Boot Time'? Remember to account for case-sensitivity.

Findstr

What it does: displays lines containing specified strings or regular expressions (Regex), from files

Why use it: to check files for specific values, string patterns, or errors, or to re-use lines containing them

How to use it:

Findstr: the basics

The 'findstr' command is a more high-powered version of the 'find' command. It looks for a specified string, or strings, in a file, or files, and displays the lines which contain a match.

It has a few more switches that relate to the position of the target text, the detail of the command output, and the sources of its own parameters. These are covered below.

It also supports a tool known as regular expressions, or 'regex'. This allows you to search for patterns in your text, rather that exact text strings. This has huge potential. It will be introduced here, but regex on its own could fill a book.

All of this means that there is a lot to 'findstr', and its section in this book is far larger than those of the last few commands.

Findstr: position switches

The '/b', '/e' and '/x' switches stand for 'beginning', 'end' and 'exact'. They refer to the position of the target string in the line of text.

Create a file and type three lines in it: 'target other text', 'other text target', and 'target'. Run the command 'Findstr target file1.txt' with each of the above switches to see the results. If you are not sure where to place the switches in the command, check the help with 'findstr /?', or just try it and see.

You may find that the '/e' and '/x' switches do not display the last line, 'target'. If so, open you file and put a blank line after 'target'. Run you command again and it will work. This shows you how the command really works. When the command looks for text that matches the end of a line, which it must also do for exact matches, it really looks for a line-break character. This tells it the line has ended. It does not accept the end-of-file character, as you have just seen. Knowing this could save you some debugging time when making batch scripts.

Note that 'findstr' does not need to its search string enclosed in double quotes, as 'find' does, unless the string has spaces.

Exercise: searching command output better (justOS.bat)

Can you make 'findstr' get only information about the operating system from 'systeminfo'? You can if you know that those lines start with the letters 'OS'. Try this now. If you do it right, you won't get any unwanted extras, like 'BIOS' information, appearing, just because they contain OS somewhere in the line.

Findstr: the switches from 'find'

The '/v', '/n' and '/i' switches do the same things as they would in the 'find' command. Respectively, they specify: displaying lines which do not match, displaying line numbers, and turning off case-sensitivity.

Findstr: the detail switches

For more detail, The '/o' or 'offset' switch displays not only the line containing the target string, but also the position of the string within the file. It displays how far into the file the target string begins, measured by the number of characters preceding it.

For less detail, the '/m' switch displays only the file name, or a list of file names, if several files contain the target string. This could be useful for piping those file names off to another command, i.e. to process only files containing your target text.

If you have not done so already, try out the '/m' and '/o' switches now.

Findstr: searching for alternatives
Create a second file and type two lines 'wall paper' and 'paper wall'. Run 'findstr "target paper" file1.txt file2.txt'. This is how to search for multiple words in multiple files using input from just the command line. You will see that the command displays lines from either file that contain either of the words you put inside the double quotes.

Note: if the first line of file two has attached itself to the last line of file one, it's the same issue as explained earlier: no blank line at the end of the file.

Findstr: getting parameters from files
You can also specify that the command should take its parameters from files too.

If you have a whole list of files to search, or a list of words to search for, you may want to store them in a file. That way, any changes to the list can be saved, and you can just have the command refer to the file holding it.

Create a file called 'FileList.txt' and give it two lines: 'file1.txt' and 'file2.txt'. Create a file called 'SearchTerms.txt' and put 'target' and 'paper' on lines one and two.

Run 'findstr /f:FileList.txt /g:SearchTerms.txt'. You will see the same lines of text displayed as in the last example. The command effectively read inside the two new files and used their contents to complete itself, so it could perform the real search.

Findstr: subdirectories
Create a folder. Inside it create a text file. Inside that type the line 'here is a target'. Make a copy of the folder.

The '/s' switch does the same here as it does in most commands: it makes the command apply to subdirectories. Run 'findstr target *' to search all files in the current directory. Run 'findstr /s target *' to search all files in the current directory and the subdirectories. Once again, each result may not get its own line. The '*' wildcard allows the command to search all files.

Findstr: finding multiple words together

If you want to search for strings with spaces in, use the '/c:' switch and the double quotes. Run 'findstr /c: "paper wall" file2.txt' and compare it to what you get without using the '/c:' switch before the quoted words.

Findstr: regex switches

The last two switches covered here are the '/l' and '/r' switches. They set the command to use the search string as a 'literal' or 'Regex'. The regex mode is the default. So the '/r' is not normally needed.

Regex can do so much that it is divided into several sections here, with exercises to understand the various options available, and how to combine them.

Regex: repeated and optional characters

Enter the lines 'color' and 'colour' into file one. Run 'findstr colou*r file1.txt'. You will see that both the US and UK spellings are displayed. The '*' character (asterisk) makes the command search for any number of occurrences of the character before itself, including zero occurrences. You can now search for spellings with optional letters, like 'u', or other optional characters.

Exercise – optional characters (commas.bat)

Make a file, 'test.txt'. Make a script (or just use command line) to find lines containing '1000' or '1,000' in the text file. Assume that you don't need to worry about your file containing results like '1,,000'. Type both formats of one-thousand on different lines of your text file, and some non-matching lines. Test your script on that.

Regex: wildcards

Type a new line with 'grey' into your file, and another with 'gray'. Run 'findstr gr.y file1.txt'. You will see all lines containing 'grey' or 'gray', because the '.' character is used by the regex to mean 'any letter'. Of course, this would also match 'groy', 'grry', and 'gr5y': wildcards are not always precise enough. Another option is to use character classes, which will be introduced shortly.

Regex goes a lot further than just wildcards though. The command line provides a limited set of regex tools, but they can still do a lot when used in combination.

Exercise – repeated wildcards (twoWords.bat)

Make a script to find lines which contain both the words 'alert' and 'error' in your 'test.txt' file, whether or not there are other words between them. You can assume 'alert' always comes first. Add some lines with both words, and other lines containing just one of the words, to your file. Test the script to make sure it only matches the former.

Regex: word position options

Run 'findstr "\<o" file1.txt' to search for any lines containing words that start with 'o'. Run 'findstr "r\>" file1.txt' to search for any lines containing words that end with 'r'.

Note that the options above search the start and end of words, unlike the '/b' and '/e' switches, which search the start and end of lines. However, regex gives you an option for line position too. You can use '^' and '$' to represent the beginning and end of a line.

Exercise – endings (ending.bat)

Make a script to find lines in 'test.txt' where the last character is a '1'. Add text to your test file and test your script in the usual way.

Exercise – beginnings (beginning.bat)
Make another script to find lines where the first character is a '2'. Test it as before.

Regex: character classes and ranges
To search for spellings with alternate characters, you can use character classes. For example, enter the lines 'license' and 'licence' then run 'findstr licen[sc]e file1.txt'. You can now search for both types of alternate spellings. You could do the same with 'grey' and 'gray'.

You can also specify a range of characters in a class, such as '[a-z]', '[A-Z]' or '[0-9]' which include all the characters in between. Another option is to use '^' (inside the brackets) to exclude characters from matching, e.g. '[^aeiou]' will match any character except a vowel and [^0-9] will exclude numbers.

For example, using character classes, you could match the characters: 'update[1-5] complete'. This would find any line with these words, and a single number up to five after 'update'. If you wanted to match this phrase with numbers twenty to twenty-five you would use: 'update2[0-5] complete'.

Exercise –ranges (endInDigit.bat, endIn1Digit.bat)
Make a script to find lines ending in a number (digit).

Make a script to find lines ending in a single-digit number, i.e. a digit with a non-digit just before it.

Exercise – numbers only (zipCode.bat)
Make a script to find lines containing only a five-digit number, like a zip code, and nothing else.

Exercise – labels only (labelsOnly.bat)
Make a script to find labels, but not comments, in a batch script. Labels (which will be introduced fully, later) start the line with ':',

comments start the line with '::' or 'REM'. Make a batch file containing all these, to test your script on. Alternatively, add comments and labels to your original script and test it on itself. This second alternative is the one provided in the answers. Warning: do not call this (or any) batch file 'label'. There is already a 'label' command which can make changes to your disk if run, e.g. by typing its name into command line.

Regex: taking characters literally

Using these regex characters in a search provides a lot of flexibility, but what if you need to match an actual '.' or '*' or '$'?

The answer is to identify them as literal characters for the computer (escape them). The escape character is '\' (backslash) and it is used before the regex character which it escapes, e.g. use '\$' to represent an actual dollar sign.

Add the lines 'I got this great book for under $10.' and 'I should totally give it a good review.' to your file. Run 'findstr \$ file1.txt' to see the first line displayed. Alternatively, if you want the whole search string to be taken literally, use the '/L' switch. This avoids the need to escape regex characters individually. Run 'findstr /L $10. file1.txt' and you will see that this works too.

Exercise – escaping (getCSVs.bat)

Make a script to find lines referring to CSV file names. Match the extension.

Regex: why use the R switch?

You might now be thinking that the '/r' switch would never be used, since the command defaults to regex mode unless you use '/l' to change it to literal.

Not so: the command will default to literal mode in one situation, meaning you need the '/r' switch to override the default in that case. If you use the '/c:' switch, the search string which follows it is taken literally by the command, including any spaces and regex characters. You will see this effect if you run 'findstr /c: "und.r $10" file1.txt'. You don't get any matches, because the '.' is not treated as a wildcard. Run 'findstr /r /c: "und.r $10" file1.txt' to see the command work. This combination allows you to use regex in a search for strings that also contains spaces.

Exercise – A tricky end (trickyEnd.bat)
Make a script to find lines in 'test.txt' where the second-last character is a space. Add text to your file and test your script in the usual way.

Conclusion
This has been a very brief introduction to regex. There are whole books written on regex, so there is a lot more potential for their use than this section covers. They can be used to match telephone numbers or post codes, for example. They can also match patterns, such as those found in certain file formats like html, e.g. to search for particular html tags.

Regex is a tool included in many scripting and programming languages, and often uses similar syntax between these, meaning skills in regex transfer well across many technologies. There are many good regex tutorials on the internet, such as at www.regexone.com.

There are some other switches available for 'findstr', which you can find by running 'findstr /?' to view the help.

FC
What it does: compares files for differences on a line-by-line basis.

Why use it: to compare similar files to see what is different, e.g. between a working and a malfunctioning system, or to check files against backups, to see what has changed

How to use it:

Note: while 'fc' is included in this chapter for completeness, it is a more specialised command than the others so far. It is probably only worth learning about if you have a specific need to compare the contents of pairs of files. Otherwise, you may prefer to skip over it, and the related command 'comp', and go straight to the next chapter.

FC: the basics

Create a text file and type four lines of text in it, i.e. type 'Line 1' on the first line, 'Line 2' on the second, and so on. Make a copy of the text file.

Run 'fc file1.txt file2.txt'. You will see the message that command prompt displays when two files are the same. To see what happens when the files are different, edit file two to have a lower case 'l' in line three and run the same command again.

The 'fc' command finds lines which differ between files. If it finds a difference on one line, it reports the whole line for both files. So you should expect to see line three in your results.

This time, however, you see lines two, three and four for each file, displayed under the file names. Even though lines two and four are clearly the same in both files, they are displayed too. This is because they are the lines directly before and after the mismatched line.

FC: comparison switches

There are a number of switches for this command.

Run 'fc /c file1.txt file2.txt' to see the comparison come up with 'no differences' once again. The '/c' switch makes the comparison case-insensitive, so it does not register that 'l' and 'L' are different.

Run 'fc /n file1.txt file2.txt' to see the command output line numbers along with the text displayed.

In file two, add three blank lines between lines two and three. Run 'fc /c /n file1.txt file2.txt'. This command should ignore the lowercase 'l' but find the blank lines.

You will see that once again the lines which differ have been identified. Lines two and three are again displayed, for both files, as the lines before and after the difference caused by the blank lines.

If the command was directly comparing the two files line-by-line, this would not happen. Once the files were out of sync, every line from the blank ones onwards would fail to match the same number line in the other file, as the line numbers in our example make clear.

However, this is not how 'fc' works. The 'fc' command re-synchronises after finding differences. This means it continues reading after any inserted (or non-deleted) lines, to find where the files start matching again. When it has done so, it continues comparing lines of text as before, even though their lines numbers no may longer match.

Run 'fc /c /w file1.txt file2.txt'. Once again, the command tells you there were no differences. The '/w' switch makes the command compress white space during comparison. Effectively, multiple spaces, tabs, or new lines are treated as single versions of themselves for comparison. As this example shows, the three line-returns, between lines '2' and '4' of file two, were treated as one line-return and so 'matched' file one. This could be a useful for comparing files such as HTML, CSS or JavaScript files, where white space is included mainly for readability and does not affect the function of the code.

99

FC: re-synchronising switches

Now, run the command again without the '/w', so that the blank lines are counted as differences, and with the switch '/lb 2'. So run 'fc /c /lb 1 file1.txt file2.txt'.

The output will display the error, but will also tell you that the 'resync' failed as the files are too different. Effectively, the command gives up: it stops comparing more lines. Run the command using switches from '/lb 2' to '/lb 5', noting the point at which the comparison does get back in sync.

The '/lb number' switch is the 'line buffer' of the comparison. It tells the command how many lines to compare before giving up on re-synchronising files. Otherwise the default value is one hundred lines.

You might have expected the files to re-synchronise at '/lb 3', but the command needs to read the matching lines, as well as the mismatched ones, otherwise what does it re-synchronise with?

The last switch covered here is '/nnnn'. It tells the command how many lines must match for re-synchronisation to occur. The default is two

To see it effect, first make both text files have nine lines each: 'line 1', 'line 2', etc. In file two, make line three end in 'a' and line seven end in 'z'. Save and exit.

So now you have files with two mismatched lines, but enough lines in between those for the command to re-synchronise the comparison.

Run 'fc file1.txt file2.txt'. As you will see, this gives you two separate sets of results: one for the first mismatch, another for the second. The command recognised that the files started matching again between lines three and seven.

Run 'fc /3 file1.txt file2.txt'. This gives the same result: there are three matching lines between the differing ones. Now run 'fc /4 file1.txt file2.txt'. This time the command cannot resynchronise between the mismatches. What happens?

Answer: one big mismatch is displayed, with all the lines in between included.

The command does not close the mismatch, until the specified number of matching lines is found, so new mismatches get added to earlier ones, and the count of matching lines is reset to zero.

There are some other switches available: run 'fc /?' to see their details.

Comp

What it does: finds single character differences between files

Why use it: to find where similar files differ on a line, especially useful with single-line files

Note: If the command alone is typed, it asks for two files to compare, pressing enter, then 'N' at the 'compare more files' prompt will end the command without it doing anything.

Note: again, this is a more specialist command, so you may wish to skip it, or leave it for last.

Comp: the basics

Create a file and in it, type 'here is some text' on line one and 'here is some more' on line two. Make a copy of the file and rename it, i.e. to 'file2'.

Run 'comp file1.txt file2.txt'. You will see a message that the 'Files compare OK' i.e. that they are the same. You will be prompted to compare more files. Press N for no and then press return.

Now open file two and replace every 's' with a 'z', so that the copy has four differences to the original. Also, change the first letter ('h') in file two to a capital 'H'.

Run 'comp file1.txt file2.txt'. You will see a message that errors have been found at various 'offsets' and, for each error, the name of both files with a code made up of numbers and letters.

The codes and offsets are in hexadecimal format by default. While normal (decimal) numbers run from nought to nine, i.e. ten digits, these hexadecimal numbers run from nought through nine, then A, B, C, D, and E to F, i.e. each digit hold values from 0-15.

To get something a bit more user friendly, you can override the defaults.

Run 'comp /a file1.txt file2.txt'. You will see that the errors listed are now letters, the ones you changed between the two files. The capital 'H' versus lower case 'h' is reported too, although you could use the '/c' switch to exclude case-sensitive differences if you wanted.

Notice that the error offsets are zero, six and eight, and so on, i.e. the number of characters away from the start of the file. The 'comp' command reads the file as one long string of characters and reports an error's position by the number of characters read before it occurs. So if the first character was different, the error would be at offset zero, for the second character, offset one, and so on.

It does not give line numbers however. To make it do that, run it with the '/L' switch, i.e. 'comp /a /l file1.txt file2.txt'. Now you get the line numbers, instead of the offset.

You might think it is always more useful to have line numbers than a hexadecimal text offset that you have to do math to convert into a number you can use to find your error. It isn't. Consider that some files, like XML files, for example, may not contain line-break characters, i.e. they can contain one, very long, line. In this case, the offset would be infinitely more useful, even if you had to convert that hexadecimal number to make use of it.

Comp: files of different sizes

Now open file two and change 'more' into 'more text'. Try to compare them. See what happens.

You should get the error message: 'Files are different sizes'.

Now that you have added some more characters to the end of one file, the command doesn't work. It only works on files of exactly the same length, unless you use '/n='. Try running 'comp /a /l /n=1 file1.txt file2.txt'.

By only comparing the specified number of lines, i.e. one line, from the beginning of the file, the command continues to work as normal for that part of the text. However, add a few characters on the end of line one in either file, and run the command again, and you will see that the 'comp' command does not detect all the extra characters when the lines are of different lengths, either. This behaviour is not documented in the help information for the command.

Finally, if you are using the command in a batch file, you might not want the prompt to pause it as it runs. You can use 'echo n' to pass through the prompt. Try running 'echo n| comp /a /l /n=1 file1.txt file2.txt' and see what happens.

Changing course in a script

So far, the batch scripts in this course have contained lists of commands, to be run in the order they appear. Sometimes, you may want a batch script to run command in a different order.

For example, you may have a script that interacts with another machine, across a network. If the script can't connect to the machine, then it can't interact. In that case, your computer may as well skip to the end of the script. It can then tell the user why it failed, without them waiting for it to fail the subsequent steps too. You could do this by putting all of the steps inside an if-clause, but if you have multiple if-clauses, and try to nest them all inside each other, this could make your script hard to read.

Similarly, you may have a script that restarts another machine, then interacts with it some more. In this case, your script needs to keep trying to connect after the restart, until the remote machine has loaded up enough to allow this. It needs to wait a while after each failure, and then go back again to the step where it tries to connect. When it connects, then it can move on.

Another situation where you need the script to go back a few steps is when it asks the user for input and they enter something invalid. For example, if the script asks them to choose from options '1' to '3', and they enter '4', or nothing at all, you need the script to ask again.

All of these examples can be handled with one command: the 'goto' command.

Goto
What it does: Move to a specified label in the batch file, from which the code continues to run.

Why use it: to skip over code, in cases where it doesn't need be to run; to go to the start of code that needs to be run again.

How to use it:

Goto: skipping steps
Follow the instructions below for a brief demonstration of how 'goto' works.

Create a batch file called 'skip.bat'. In it, enter the following lines:

> @ECHO OFF
>
> IF %1==skip GOTO END
>
> > ECHO You entered: %1
>
> :END
>
> ECHO The End!
>
> PAUSE

The ':END' part of the script is a label. Labels are used to mark a position in a script. The 'GOTO' command, followed by the label's name, is used to jump to that position. The script then continues running from there.

Save the batch file. In the command window, navigate to its directory: 'Goto1'. Run the batch script with any word as a parameter, e.g. run 'skip hello'. You will see your parameter displayed. Now run it with the word 'skip' as the parameter, i.e. 'skip skip'. You will see that this example does not display your parameter.

Used this way, the 'goto' command allows you to run commands conditionally. Effectively, you state the condition(s) under which a section of script is skipped over. These conditions do not have to be based on user input. For example, you could have a script check if a file exists, before trying to process it.

Goto: choosing from two options

To make a script run different code for each case, rather than none in one case, see this next example.

Create a batch file called 'decide.bat'. Enter the following lines:

```
@ECHO OFF
IF %1==2 GOTO PART2
    :PART1
        ECHO Running part 1 code
        GOTO END
    :PART2
        ECHO Running part 2 code
:END
ECHO Process complete!
PAUSE
```

Run this command with the parameter '2', then with any other parameter. Used this way, the 'goto' command allows you to run different blocks of code according to whether a condition is met. In this case, the script always runs your first piece of (dummy) code, unless you tell it to run the second piece.

Note how part one contains a 'goto' command to skip over part two. Otherwise, running part one would run part two afterwards. Scripts continue to the next command down by default, unless you tell them otherwise.

Goto: choosing from multiple options

The 'goto' command can also make decisions in a way that is both simpler, and more powerful, than 'if'. This next example leaves 'if' and its 'either...or' decision-making behind. Other languages would use 'switch...case' or 'select...case' to decide between multiple options. Batch has a different way.

Create a batch file called 'select.bat' and in it type:

```
@ECHO OFF

GOTO CASE%1

    :CASE1

        ECHO Running code for case 1 (reporting on files)

        GOTO END

    :CASE2

        ECHO Running code for case 2 (backing up files)

        GOTO END

    :CASE3

        ECHO Running code for case 3 (scanning system logs)

:END

ECHO Process complete!

PAUSE
```

Run 'select' with each parameter from 1 to 3. You should see your code run for each case.

The parameter is used to complete the label name, so you only need one 'GOTO' at the start of the script, no matter how many options you give the user.

Goto: looping
The final technique covered here is the backwards jump. Using 'goto' to jump backwards in the code allows repetition i.e. looping.

Create a batch file called 'repeat' and in it type:

```
@ECHO OFF

SET Lines=0

:START

    REM add one to the count of lines

    SET /A Lines+=1

    REM add a line of text to the end of a file

    ECHO dummy text line %Lines%>> file1.txt

    REM if fewer lines have been added than the   user asked for, repeat the last two steps

IF %Lines% LSS %1 GOTO START

PAUSE
```

Run 'repeat 3'. Now open your text file and see the result. It should contain three lines. Run 'repeat 10' and check again. It should now contain ten lines. You have just created a batch script for quickly generating a dummy data file of any size you specify. You may find this useful when testing scripts you design later, especially if you want to test them on a large file to measure their speed.

You can also use the 'for' command for looping. In fact, the use of 'goto' at all is generally discouraged in programming. It is so flexible that it makes it easy to write code without any structure, code that jumps all over the place and is hard to follow. In batch script, however, 'goto' loops are one of only two loop types available, apart from recursion. Being able to use 'goto' loops is therefore useful.

Exercise – checking for user input (checkInput.bat)
Make a batch script that asks a user for input, i.e. to type something and press return. When they press return, it should check whether they typed anything. If so, it should report what they typed. If not, it should ask for input again.

Exercise – making dummy files (makeDummy.bat)
Make a batch script that allows users to create dummy files for testing other scripts or programs on. Make it give the user a choice of file types to create: text, CSV, and html. Present the types as a numbered list, and prompt the user to enter a number to create a file of that type. Have the script loop round at the end so the user can create as many files of each type as they need.

As you need to be able to create multiple files of the same type, you need a way to give them different names, so they don't just overwrite each other. One way to do this would be to have a variable that increases by one each time, and add the number to the end of the file names. However, if you closed and opened the script's command window, the variable would lose count and start again. To make your script more robust, have the script add the time to the files' names, as it creates them. This will make each new file name unique.

As the variable '%time%' contains ':' and '.' characters, which are invalid in file names, you will also need to store its value in another variable, which you can then process to remove those characters from the string, before adding what's left to your file name.

This may sound like a lot, but it doesn't take too many lines of code to do. It does draw from material covered earlier in the course, such as string processing, so you make need to refer to 'set' in book 1. To make the script easier to develop, make it as described in the first paragraph above, and, once you have that working, add the time feature in. Also, to simplify this exercise, don't include validation, e.g. of user input, unless you really want to.

More about variables

There is more to learn about variables. Are they stored in the command window, or the script? What happens to them when the script finishes? How do you use one variable to change the string of another?

All this, and why it matters, is covered below. This section can help you do more with batch script, and do it more reliably.

Setlocal

What it does: prevents scripts accessing subroutine variables, or the command window accessing script variables. It can also turn delayed expansion of variables on or off. The concept of delayed expansion will be explained more fully below.

Why use it: To allow more reliable use of scripts and subroutines by eliminating a potential source of error.

How to use it:

The 'setlocal' command allows you to contain variables within a script, or within a subsection of that script. This prevents the command window, and other parts of the script, from accessing them, and helps ensure that variables are used only as intended.

To see how it works, create the script below, save it as 'local.bat' and run it.

```
@ECHO OFF

ECHO %var1%

SETLOCAL

SET var1=local variable

ECHO %var1%
```

ENDLOCAL

ECHO %var1%

PAUSE

Running this command will output line one as 'echo is off', which is the output you get for running 'echo' with a non-existent variable. Line two will output as the variable's text. Line three will also output as 'echo is off', even though the variable has already been set. This is because, outside of the 'SETLOCAL…ENDLOCAL' block, the variable does not exist, at least as far as the computer knows. The variable is contained to one part of the script, meaning you cannot accidentally set or use it elsewhere.

This is also a good opportunity to show how variables linger in the command window. Run this script from the command line, and then run 'echo %var1%'. You will get the result '%var1%', indicating the command window could not find the variable, so it just outputted the text you gave it.

Now take out, or comment out, the 'setlocal' and 'endlocal' parts of the script. Also, make it set 'var1' to 'not local'. Run the script again, then run 'echo %var1%'. This time, you get the variable's value: the script has passed the variable back to the command window. Without 'setlocal' the variable has outlived the script. If you ran the script again, its variable would then have a pre-set value, which could change how the script worked.

While using 'setlocal', or not, in a script often doesn't affect the outcome, it can do. If two scripts, or the same script run twice, are setting and using variables in the command window, with the same names, then they can use or set each other's values. The scripts would then run using completely unexpected parameters.

The use of 'setlocal' is also important when using the 'call' command to pass variables to subroutines. That will be covered in the 'call' command section in book three.

Setlocal: parameters

The 'setlocal' command also has two pairs of parameters. The first pair is 'enable extensions' and 'disable extensions'. In batch script, these are written without spaces, and usually in capital letters. As their names suggest, they turn command extensions on or off. The help documentation of some commands states that certain features, like some switches or comparison operators, are only available when command extensions are turned on (enabled). Fortunately, command extensions are enabled by default, so do not need to be turned on, unless they have been deliberately turned off.

The second pair of parameters is 'enable delayed expansion' and 'disable delayed expansion'. Like the last pair, these are written without spaces, and usually in capital letters. Unlike command extensions however, delayed expansion is turned off (disabled) by default, so you will need to turn it on with 'setlocal' before you can use it.

So what is delayed expansion? What is expansion, even, and why would you delay it?

Normal expansion

Normally, if you use variables in a script, you mark them out with '%' signs, as below:

    ECHO %myVariable%

The computer then reads through the text and replaces the marked out variable name with its contents. So if your variable held '5', it would make:

ECHO 5

This is called expansion. The variable has been expanded to its value.

At this point, the command line runs the code, e.g. 'echo 5', and outputs the result, e.g. '5'. This is normal expansion, i.e. it is not delayed.

Delayed expansion

If you enable delayed expansion, the command line reads through the code at runtime. It looks for variables marked out as follows:

!otherVariable!

If it finds any, these variables are expanded then, as the code is run. This is the delay. To see how delayed expansion can be used, here are some examples to run as batch files:

    @ECHO OFF

    SET item1=pizza

    SET item2=lemonade

    SET item3=salad

    SETLOCAL ENABLEDELAYEDEXPANSION

    ECHO !item%1!

    PAUSE

Save the script as 'item.bat'. Run it from the command line by running 'item 1', then 'item 2', then 'item 3', to see the results. This script works because '%1' is expanded, and completes the name of the 'item' variable, before that variable is expanded too. To see how this works in the command window, remove or comment out the '@ECHO OFF' line in 'item.bat' and run the script again. Notice what appears at the command prompt in the 'echo' statement.

If you use this technique with 'goto' and labels instead of 'echo' and strings, you can control the path taken through a script.

Working with strings

So, you can use delayed expansion to make one variable form part of another's name, as in the script above. Equally, you can use it to modify the string value of one variable with another, as follows:

> SET var1=motor
>
> SET var2=vintage motorcar parts
>
> SETLOCAL ENABLEDELAYEDEXPANSION
>
> ECHO !var2:%var1%=!
>
> PAUSE

The script above displays the text of variable two, with the text of variable one removed, i.e. without the word 'motor'.

There is no '@ECHO OFF' in this script, so if you run it, you can also see the commands as they appear after normal expansion, but before delayed expansion, i.e. 'echo !var2:motor=!'.

The point here is that if you want to use one variable's value inside another's, as with the string replacement, you use delayed expansion.

Delayed expansion also helps when working with variables inside 'for' loops. Book three covers that topic.

Endlocal

What it does: closes the variable-containing block opened by 'setlocal'

Why use it: as with 'setlocal', to help prevent errors

How to use it:

This command ends a block of commands using 'local' variables. It terminates the self-contained environment for variable handling, established by the previous 'setlocal' command. For examples, see the scripts in the 'setlocal' section.

Exercise – a string replace 'function' (stringReplace.bat)

There aren't really functions in command line, but you can make a script that processes parameters as input, and outputs a string using 'echo'.

Make a script that runs from command line and takes three string parameters. Make it replace the first string with the second, inside the third. For example, 'stringReplace hello hi "hello there"' would come out as 'hi there'.

Use delayed expansion for this. The parameters, '%1', '%2', and '%3', are processed by normal expansion, so if you need to delay the expansion of one of their strings, assign its value to another variable and expand that instead.

Exercise – make dummy files differently (makeDummy2.bat)

Copy your 'makeDummy.bat' file, or start a fresh version. Use delayed expansion to make the script do the same thing, but without using 'goto' to move between options. You can use the same approach as the menu items (pizza, etc) script earlier: define you variables and use the number the user enters to make their names, which you then expand again.

Knowing when to quit

Some batch scripts do nothing more than run a few commands and then stop. The script reaches the end of the batch file and ends that way. Other batch scripts provide a variety of ways to run their code, skipping or including certain sections in the file. In these cases, you can use a command like 'exit' to stop the script. That way, the script can end in each case, whether or not the last section to run brings it to the end of the file.

Exit

What it does: ends a batch file and (optionally) returns an error code

Why use it: To end programs part way through, under specified conditions. For example, if the user does not enter the correct input, a child script (one started by another script/program) could return an error code. The parent script could then translate that into 'error: input missing', for the user's benefit.

How to use it:

The need for 'exit'

Batch scripts often have an if-clause, allowing the system to follow different paths through them, depending on the conditions it finds. For a simple example of this, create a batch file using the text below and name it 'info.bat'.

```
@ECHO OFF

GOTO %1

  :TD

      ECHO It is %time% on %date%.

  :OU
```

        ECHO You are running %OS% as
    %username%

    PAUSE

Now, run it from the command line: use 'info ou', then 'info td'.

The system takes your parameter, 'ou' or 'td', and uses it as '%1'. The 'goto' command sends it to the label which '%1' matches, and the system runs the commands from there on. You will notice that entering 'td' runs not only the 'td' command section, but also the 'ou' command section. In this case, 'TD' stands for 'Time and Date', so the batch script should display those and stop. The system, however, just keeps reading down the script by default. To make it stop early, use the 'exit' command.

Exiting
Add 'EXIT' in a new line, above ':OU', in the script. Add 'PAUSE' above 'EXIT', so that the script allows you to see its result, before exiting. Run the script again using 'info td', and press a key when prompted, so the script can run its course.

Did your command window shut down? That is inconvenient. Worse, if your batch script had been a child script, shutting down the command window would have stopped the parent script too. This would derail your automated process part way through and leave you to clear up the mess. Why did this happen? If you already ran 'exit' in the command line, you may have some idea. If not, do that now.

The 'exit' command exits the command window, not just the batch script that the window is running. In some cases, this is useful. If your batch script opens other command windows to run commands in those, you may want to shut those extras down using 'exit'. In this case, running a script in the original window, you probably want to keep using the window open afterwards. You need the '/b' switch.

Exiting just the script

The '/b' switch exits only the current batch script. Add it to your batch script, so that it reads 'EXIT /B'. Run the command 'info td' again. You will now see your command window stay open. This is more than convenient. It also allows you to use another feature of 'exit': the exit code, or error level.

Exit codes: how they work

The exit code parameter allows a script to send an integer (whole number) code to its parent. If there are multiple exit points in the script, each can have its own error code to output if used. It does this by setting the command window's %errorlevel% variable. This allows the script to tell the user, or the program, running it, if anything went wrong, and what that was, according to which exit point was used.

To see some examples of error levels, run 'echo lalala' then 'echo %errorlevel%'. You should see '0' i.e. 'no error'. Now run 'type lalala.txt' and check the error message, then 'echo %errorlevel%' to see the code number for this error. Run 'lalala' and do the same.

The command window keeps the last error level that was set by a command or script. However, it is worth noting that a command, or script, running without error does not necessarily reset the error code to zero.

When one batch script (the parent) calls another (the child), the parent can respond to the '%errorlevel%' set from the child's exit code. This allows you to write your parent scripts to respond to problems that its child encounters. A number code is easier to use in the parent than a long error message would be: 'if

%errorlevel%==1' is easier to use than 'if %errorlevel%==The system cannot find the file specified.'

To try this out, add these two lines to 'info.bat', just below the '@ECHO OFF' line:

> SET myInput=%1
>
> IF NOT %myInput%==%myInput:~0,2% ECHO Too many letters in parameter & EXIT /B 2

The if-clause above compares the whole parameter to its first two letters. If there are more than two letters, then the two sides of '==' are 'NOT' the same, so the user's input must be wrong, and the rest of the line runs.

So, the script now checks that the parameter has two letters, no more. If the parameter is too long, it returns an error code for any parent scripts, and an error message for any users.

Run 'info abc' then 'echo %errorlevel%' to see how this works.

Error codes: why they matter

A potential use of error codes is as follows. You want to run a process on a lot of files. You have a script to do it for you, but maybe you didn't write it yourself. Sometimes the script fails part way through changing a file, so you have to back up the files before running it. Then you have to check it worked on each file, and restore them from the backups if not. This of course breaks the automation, meaning extra work for you.

To avoid this, you create a parent script which backs up the files then runs the original script on each of them. If the child script runs without error, the parent deletes the backup. If not, the parent copies the backup file onto the original, overwriting it and fixing any problems the child may have left. The child script reports its success or failure, and the type of failure, to the parent through an exit code.

Not only does this automate the process, but you get a list of cases where the child failed and the reasons why. With this knowledge, you change the child script. By the next time you need to run it, the whole process is error-free.

Error levels and 'if'

There is a special syntax for using error levels in if-clauses. They support use of %errorlevel% without the normal comparison operators, i.e. 'IF errorlevel 2 ECHO script aborted due to bad parameters' is working code. Normally, you would expect something like '%errorlevel%==2', but the command line provides a short version just for error levels.

File and Folder operations

So far, this course has covered two main areas of command use: getting and processing information/data, and controlling batch scripts, i.e. automation. It has also covered creating files, writing information to files and the console, customising the console, and a few miscellaneous commands like 'shutdown' and 'chkdsk'. What it has not yet covered much of, is how to make changes on the system. It will introduce this topic now.

One of the most commonly changed parts of a computer is the file system. Files and folders can be created, deleted, renamed and moved. They also have attributes, like 'read-only' which can be changed.

The commands which do this are:

Del (erase) – to delete files

Mkdir (md) – to make new folders

Rmdir (rd) – to delete folders

Rename (ren) – to rename files

Move – to move files or rename folders, or files

Attrib – to change file or folder attributes, like 'read-only'

Note: some of the commands above have two names. You can run 'mkdir' or 'md' to the same effect, likewise 'rmdir' and 'rd', and so on.

Learn to use these commands and the copy commands in the next chapter, and you learn to control a computer's file system.

Del
What it does: deletes files

Why use it: to remove files no longer needed, i.e. those with errors, duplicates, old backups

How to use it:

Del: the basics

Using 'del' is straightforward. Try it out as follows.

Make a folder 'del1' and change directory to it. In the folder, make some files to delete: create three text files.

Run 'del file1.txt'. This deletes the file.

Run 'del /p *.txt'. See what happens.

The second example above shows two, independent, features of 'del'. Using the wildcard '*' with the '.txt' file extension makes the command process each text file in the current directory. Using the '/p' switch makes the command prompt you to confirm or reject the deletion of each file.

There is also a '/q' switch. The system, by default, prompts you to confirm certain types of deletion. Using the Q switch runs the command in 'quiet' mode, suppressing any such prompts. This is useful if you want to the command to run through without stopping to wait for user input, e.g. when designing a batch script.

If you want to delete all file types, not just those ending '.txt', you can change the wildcards to include all file names, with all extensions, i.e. 'del *.*'. Beware, however, doing this in a batch file. If your batch file is deleting all files from its own directory, as it does by default, it will also delete itself.

Deleting from subdirectories

Create a folder, and in it a text file called 'file1', inside it. Copy that file back to the parent 'del1' folder. You should now have two files with the same name.

Run 'del /s file1.txt'. You will see that the files have been deleted from both the folder and its subfolder. The new switch makes the 'del' command run on subfolders (of the current directory) too. The '/s' switch, for applying commands to subdirectories, is available in many commands, not just 'del'. However, adding '/s' to commands does not automatically work the same way. For example, adding it to the 'shutdown' command just makes the computer shutdown. Switches' behaviour is command-specific. As always, check the command's help using '/?' if in doubt.

Deleting read-only and hidden files

Create a new file and set its read-only attribute to on. To do this, right-click on the file in Explorer and select properties from the context menu that appears, then tick the read-only box. Alternatively, run 'attrib +r file1.txt' then 'attrib', if an 'R' appears before the file name, it is read-only. The 'attrib' command is covered later in this book.

Run 'del file1.txt'. The system will now block you.

Run 'del /f file1.txt' to override the file's read-only status and 'force' the system to delete the file. The '/f' switch allows you to include read-only files in the deletions, despite their status.

Create a file as before, except this time set the attributes to 'hidden' in the file properties, or use '+h' with 'attrib' in command line. If you need to unhide it for any reason, go to the 'view' menu in 'Windows Explorer' and tick the 'hidden items' box (or run 'attrib' with '–h').

Run 'del *.txt'. The system will tell you it can't find the file '*.txt'. However if you remove the hidden status and run the command again, it works. So, hidden files are protected from deletion too. To get round this, you can use the '/a:' switch.

124

Deleting files with certain attributes

The '/a:' switch allows you to specify, by file attribute, which files to delete.

To see how this works, create two text files, both hidden, with one of those read-only. Run 'attrib' and you will see both files listed, along with their attributes.

Run 'del /a:hr *.txt' to delete the hidden read-only file. After the '/a:' switch, H is for 'hidden', R is for 'read-only'. Run 'attrib' to check the deletion worked i.e. the file with both 'h' and 'r' next to its name is gone, and then create the hidden read-only file again, with the same properties.

Run 'del /a:h-r *.txt' to delete the other hidden file, the one that is not read-only. Run 'attrib' to check it worked. Putting '-' before an attribute letter makes the command exclude files with that attribute from the deletion.

So, by specifying attribute letters after the '/a:' switch, you can specify which types of files to include in, and exclude from, the deletion and only delete files which meet all of your criteria.

Rename (ren)

What it does: renames files or folders and/or changes file extensions.

Why use it: to systematically rename files or folders. It can also change the extensions of files to something the system recognises, so that it can open them.

How to use:

Ren: the basics

Create a text file. In it, on the first line, type '1,2,3' without spaces after the commas. On the second line, type '2,4,6', again without spaces after the commas. Save and close the file.

Run 'ren file.txt hisfile.txt'.

In Windows Explorer, or by running 'dir', you should now see that your file has been renamed. Your command specified the name of the file to look for and what to rename it as.

Ren: wildcards

Make a copy of the text file and save it as 'hisfile2.txt'. Run 'ren his*.txt her*.txt'. You should see the first two letters of each file name change.

The '*' symbol (asterisk) is a wildcard, meaning 'any text'. Using it makes the command apply itself to any file in the current folder with a name matching the pattern you specified, in this case that means names beginning in 'his' and ending in '.txt'.

The '.' and '\' characters will not be matched by a wildcard, as these have important roles in the file system. They separate file extensions and other folder names, respectively, from the file name. To match these characters, they must be typed as they are, e.g. to match all text files, use '*.txt' not '*txt'.

Running the command applies it to any matching file, and using the '*' means many files can be matched. The command also preserves the text matched by the wildcards, in this case 'file' and 'file2', as you will have seen from the example. However, this works differently to how you might expect.

Run 'ren her*.txt your*.txt'.

In Windows Explorer, you should now see 'yourile' and 'yourile2'. The '*' has preserved the last parts of the file names. What happened to the first letter of those parts, 'f'?

Answer: it was overwritten when the space was needed.

This does limit the ways in which you can use 'ren'. However, book three introduces the 'for' loop, which gives you a way to overcome these limits.

Ren: file extensions

Run 'ren *.txt *.csv'. This will change the extension of all text files in your folder, whilst preserving the file names. If you now look at the files in Windows Explorer, they display as CSV (Comma-Separated Values) files. By default, these open in Excel. Open one up and see how it looks. You just used command line to effectively turn your text file into a spreadsheet. If you know your way around Excel, you may be able to import text file data to a spreadsheet to the same effect, but can you do it to multiple files at once?

This technique can apply to all kinds of files and is easy to adapt and scale up. You can even save the command in a batch file, copy it to a folder full of text files, and run it, to make them all CSVs. This kind of thing puts the 'batch' in 'batch script': such a file can run the same process on many items (a batch of them), all in one go.

Ren: renaming folders

You can rename folders in the same way you rename files. Create a folder, 'folder1', and run 'ren folder1 folder2'. You will see its name change. The 'move' command, which is covered later, can also rename a folder, so there is some overlap of command functions here.

Exercise – restore a file from backup (restore.bat)

Suppose you back up a file before making some changes on it. As the 'copy' command is covered later in this book, you could just 'type' its contents into a backup file. For example, create a file called 'data.txt', enter some text in it, and use 'type data.txt>data.bak' to make the backup. The '.bak' extension is just a way of indicating the file is a backup, without moving or renaming it.

Now suppose you make some changes on the text file, but they don't work out, and you want to get rid of it and put the backup in its place, i.e. make the backup a text file. You can do this from command line in two lines, excluding '@echo off'. Can you make a batch script to do this, taking the file name, minus its extension, as a parameter?

Exercise – safely restore a file from backup (safeRestore.bat)

There is a problem with the batch script above. It deletes the original file without checking whether the backup exists to restore it from. This means that someone could try to restore a file and end up losing it.

Make the script check a backup exists before deleting the original. You can do this with the 'if' command, and the 'exist' keyword, as covered in book one. If you need a quick reminder, run 'if /?' to see the relevant help details.

Make the script end with an exit code of '1', if it doesn't find a backup file.

Call: a brief introduction

There are several ways to have one script run another. The next exercise uses the 'call' command to do so. The next book will go into depth about this topic. For now, if you want your script to run another script, just type 'call' followed by the script name in your batch file. You can put parameters after the script name as normal, e.g. 'CALL myScript myParameter'. This script will run and return an exit code (or 'error level') to its parent script, which will then continue with its own code.

Exercise – return error messages for exit codes (parent.bat)

Make a script that takes a file name as a parameter, and runs 'safeRestore.bat' with that parameter.

Have the script check the exit code that 'safeRestore' returns. Have it display an error message, or a success message, for the user.

MkDir

What it does: creates new folders

Why use it: to make new folders

How to use it:

Run 'mkdir folder1'. In Windows Explorer, you will see this appear as a folder inside your 'mkdir1' folder. If you are using the command window, run 'tree' to see an overview of these folders so far.

You just created a folder (directory).

Now run 'mkdir folder1\folder2'. In Windows Explorer, you will see the second folder appear as a subfolder inside the first. If you are using cmd.exe you would need to run 'tree' again to see this.

You just used the current directory, the default one used by command line, and the name of its subfolder together, to specify where to create your new folder.

You can refer to folders within your current folder this way, as an alternative to typing the path out in full or changing directory. This principle applies to command line in general, not just the 'mkdir' command.

Now run 'mkdir folder1\folder2a\folder3'. In the command window, run 'tree' to see an overview now. Notice that two new folders have appeared: '2a' did not exist before the command, but it does now.

You can create a whole series of folders, one inside the other, in this way.

Exercise – make folders differently (mkdirs.bat)

Make a script, to run from command line, to take three parameters. It will make folders, and name them using the parameters. Have it prompt the user whether they want to create the folders side-by-side, in the current directory, or one-inside-the-other, as in the example above.

Rmdir (rd)

What it does: deletes folders

Why use it: to remove files or folders no longer needed, i.e. those with errors, duplicates, old backups

How to use it:

Create two folders. In the second folder, create a subfolder. In the subfolder, create a file.

Run 'Rmdir folder1'. You should see that the folder no longer appears in the file system. You have deleted (removed) the directory.

Try to remove the second folder the same way. You get an error saying the folder is not empty. If you try to remove its subfolder, e.g. with 'rmdir folder2\subfolder1', which contains only a file and no more folders, you get the same result. Without switches, 'rmdir' can remove only empty directories.

Try to remove the second folder again. Use the '/S' switch this time. This time you are prompted to confirm you want to delete the folder, despite it having contents. Say 'no' to the prompt, i.e. type 'n' and press return.

Run the command again with the '/Q' switch added too. It deletes the directory without prompting. Q is for quiet. If you want the command not to prompt, e.g. in a batch file that you want to just start and leave running, use '/Q'.

Move

What it does: moves files and folders, renames folders

Why use it: to move information to another folder or drive, e.g. for storage or to do processing locally

How to use it:

Moving folders

Create two folders. Create two files in the first folder.

Run 'move folder1 folder2'. This moves the first folder into the second.

Run 'cd folder2' then 'move folder1 ..'. This moves the 'folder1' subfolder into the parent directory, which is represented by '..'. Run 'cd..' to return to the parent directory, then run 'dir' to check the move worked.

You can move files in the same way you move folders. For example, create 'file3.txt' and run 'move file3.txt folder2'. The file moves into the folder.

If you need to move a specific folder, or file, into another folder, without regard to your current directory, you can use its full path, e.g. 'C:\thisfolder\thatfolder\etc'. You can specify the destination folder the same way.

Renaming folders

There is no folder three, but run 'move folder1 folder3' anyway. Folder three will appear. Look inside it to see your text files. They are proof that folder one became folder three.

So when you 'move' a folder into a folder name that does not exist, you actually rename the folder.

Run 'move folder3*.txt folder2'. This moves the text files from folder three into folder two.

Prompt switches
The 'move' command also has a '/y' switch for suppressing, and a '/-y' switch for causing, prompts asking the user to confirm or reject the move for each file.

Exercise – restore a folder from backup (restoreDir.bat)
Make a script to restore a folder from a backup copy. The backup copy should have the same name, but with '_bak' on the end. Make the script run from command line and take the folder name as a parameter.

As with 'restore.bat', the script should delete the original folder, named in the parameter, and rename the backup to replace it. Make sure your script restores all subfolders, empty or not, and files within the folder. Assume, for the purposes of this exercise, that the folder will always have been backed up when the script is run, so there is no risk of losing it.

Attrib
What it does: gets or sets the file/folder attributes: 'read-only', 'hidden', 'archive' and 'system'

Why use it: to protect files from modification by users or programs. It can also hide files that users do not need to see, de-cluttering their view of Windows Explorer. Equally, it can find and/or unhide hidden files and unprotect read-only files.

How to use it:

Attrib: the basics

Create two folders with two files in each. Run 'attrib' from the parent directory ('attrib1'). It tells you it could not find files, i.e. it looks for files by default, not folders.

Change directory to the first folder. Run 'attrib'. Notice how it shows you the names of the files within the folder. It displays their whole file path too, which can be very long. When you are familiar with virtual drives (which you will be after book three), you may wish to use those to display a drive letter in place of the path, to make the output of 'attrib' a bit more readable.

Notice also how there is a space before each file name. This space may contain letters such as A for archive, H for hidden, R for read-only and S for system. These are the attributes of the files. The system attribute indicates that a file is critical to the working of the computer, and the archive attribute is to do with the computer's own backup processes. The other two attributes are of more interest here: read-only and hidden.

Read-only

Run 'attrib +r file1.txt'. The '+r' added the read-only status. Run 'attrib'. Notice how the file is now listed with an 'R' next to its name to show its read-only status. To test this, go to the folder in Windows Explorer and open the file. Type some text in and try to save. A 'save as' option will open and if you try to save with the same name anyway, the system will block you, advising the read-only status as the cause.

So the file can still be read and copies of it made and modified, but the original is protected from modification. It is not password protected, so someone else could turn the 'read-only' status off, but it does protect against users accidentally overwriting the file contents, which can be useful for shared documents, such as forms, which may be used by many people use on a regular basis.

For example, a shared timesheet form may be updated with an employee's hours if they forget to save their own copy before changing it. You could use 'read-only' to protect the file against this.

You can set both read-only and hidden attributes on individual files without using the command line, but with the command line you can set these attributes in bulk, i.e. for many files at once, using wildcards if necessary.

Hidden files

Run 'attrib +h file1.txt'. Run 'attrib'. Notice how the file is now listed with an 'H' next to its name: it is now hidden, as well as read-only. To test this, go to the folder in Windows Explorer and look for the file. You won't see it. Run 'Dir'. You won't see the file listed in the output there either. So hidden status hides files from the user and from some commands, protecting it from access and modification by either.

Whilst the hidden status, like the read-only status, can be overcome by users, it does help to prevent users from seeing, reading, changing or using files that you don't want them to. For example, the system hides files that are generated for use by itself, such as those which hold users profiles on a server. So users are far less likely to change or delete these files by mistake. Equally, the files do not then clutter up the file system, or at least the user's view of it.

Another potential application of this is hiding script files. Batch files are often put into a shared folder to be run, to take advantage of the fact that they process their current folder's contents by default. If the batch file is left there between uses, an unwitting user might try to open the file to see what it is. In doing so, they would cause the script to run. Hiding the file would make this far less likely to happen.

Removing attributes

Now run 'attrib –r –h file1.txt'. Run 'attrib'. Notice that the file returns to normal, i.e. not hidden or read-only. So the attributes represented by the various letters can be set or unset, i.e. turned on and off, using plus or minus signs before those letters.

Attrib: without file names and with wildcards

Run 'attrib +r' then 'attrib'. Both files are now read-only. If you don't use a file name, 'attrib' applies itself to all the files in the current directory.

Change directory to the second folder in attrib1. Run 'attrib +h *1.txt' to hide any text files ending in '1'.

Attrib: subfolders

Return to your 'attrib1' folder and run 'attrib /s' to see all your files and their attributes, from both folders. Using '/s' makes your command look in subfolders.

Run 'attrib +h /d /s folder1'. Using '/s' with '/d' allows you to see or change the folder attributes as well. This command will hide the folder.

Exercise – Clearing attributes (clearAll.bat)

Now, can you clear those R and H attributes from the files and folders in one command? Have a go. You can check if it worked with 'attrib /s /d'

Copying files and folders

Copying files and folders is a common task. You may do it within one machine, as part of a backing up process. You may do it between machines, as part of a fix or update, using the contents of a working or up-to-date machine to change the contents of the others.

This chapter introduces three such commands: 'copy', 'replace', and 'xcopy'.

Copy

What is does: copies files to new folders, or to new filenames, or both.

Why use it: to backup files, or to copy the contents of several files into one

How to use it:

Copy: the basics

Inside the folder 'copy1', create a text file and a folder. Use the usual names, 'file1.txt' and 'folder1'.

Run 'copy file1.txt file2.txt'. You will see the second file appear. You just made a named copy of a file, inside the same folder.

Run 'copy file1.txt folder1'. You just copied the file to that folder. As the source file and destination folder are both in the current directory, the folder name is enough for the command to work. If you wanted to copy the file outside of the current directory, the normal rules apply: you would replace 'folder1' with a full path, e.g. 'C:\Users\John\Documents\MyCopies'.

Exercise – new name, new folder (myCopy.bat)

How would you copy file one to folder one and give the copy a new name as you do so? Have a go. Make the copy appear as 'NewName.txt'.

Overwriting and prompting

The 'copy' command overwrites files in the destination folder if they have the same name as the copy.

The 'copy' command will also, in some cases, prompt the user to confirm that they want to copy a file. This default behaviour can be overridden using switches. The '/y' switch suppresses prompts in the command. The '/-y' switch makes them appear.

Consolidating files

Now put some different text in files one and two, in your main folder ('copy1'). Run 'copy file1.txt + file2.txt file3.txt'. Open the third file and you will see that the text from file one has been copied into it and file two's text added to the end (appended). This technique of specifying multiple source files with '+', and only one destination file name, combines all of the source files' contents into that one destination file. With wildcards, the same technique can be used on a larger or unknown number of source files.

Copying multiple files

For an example of copying multiple files, without combining them, type 'copy folder1*.txt' in the command window. Putting the '*' in the source file name means any text files in the specified subfolder will be copied. Not specifying a destination file name means the files keep their original name(s) when copied. Now, run the command. It will prompt you about replacing 'file1', as you didn't use the '/y' switch. Then it will say that two files were copied, although, as one replaced a file in the destination, this may not be obvious in Windows Explorer.

You should now see the file 'NewName.txt' in your main folder, alongside 'file1.txt' and the others. If you open 'file1.txt' you will see that the text is gone, because the copy that replaced it never had text.

Question
Why do you think these files appeared in the main folder?

Answer
The main folder is the current directory, from which you ran the command. Not specifying a directory meant the current one was used as the destination folder by default, so this is where the copies appeared.

Exercise – backup multiple files (backup.bat)
Make a script which use 'copy' to backup any and all text files in a folder, so that they have '.bak' extensions.

Exercise – restore multiple files (restoreAll.bat)
Make a script, or change your 'restore.bat' file, to restore all those files you just backed up, from their '.bak' versions. It should delete the text files and rename the backup versions.

Exercise – safely restore multiple files (safeRestoreAll.bat)
The above script isn't very good. It deletes files which may not be backed up. Make a new version, using the 'copy' command, to overwrite text files with backups of the same name, if they exist. The command has a switch for this, so you will not need 'if exist'. Then have the script delete the '.bak' files.

Replace
What it does: replaces files with other files of the same name, or adds (copies) files to a new folder.

Why use it: to replace old files with updated versions, or to selectively back up files

How to use it:

Replace: the basics

Create a folder and a text file inside that ('file1.txt'). Write some text in the file. Make a copy of the folder, including its contents. Type something else inside the copy's text file. Create a second text file ('file2.txt') in the copied folder.

Run 'replace folder1*.txt folder2'. Check inside the copy's text file and you will find it matches the original. You just replaced the copied file in folder two with the original from folder one. The command matched files in the two folders by name, before replacing them. It ignored the unmatched file ('file2.txt').

Add the '/p' switch and run the command again, i.e. 'replace /p folder1*.txt folder2'. This will prompt you to confirm, for each file, that you do want to replace it. This also takes you through which files the command is handling and in what order, should you need to know.

Replace: subfolders

Add a subfolder into your copied folder ('folder2'). Add a file in that, with the same name as your original file ('file1.txt'). Add some unique text into that, e.g. 'this file is in the subfolder', and run the last command again. You will see from the prompts that files in subfolders are not included in the 'replaceable' list.

Run the command with the '/s' switch to include subfolder files, so that they are replaced too, i.e. 'replace /p /s folder1*.txt folder2'. You will see the file replaced this time. You can verify this by checking the file contents to see if they changed, as you can with the other examples for this command.

Replace: adding files
There are two switches which affect the way this command replaces files. So far, this command has literally 'replaced' files. It can do more.

Create a new file, with a totally new name, like 'file3.txt', in folder one. Change the contents of file one in folder two again. Now run the command with the '/a' switch, i.e. 'replace /a /p folder1*.txt folder2'.

You will see that file one is not replaced, i.e. you are not prompted about it and its text remains unchanged, whereas the new file is copied over to folder two. The A is for 'Add'. Using this switch effectively reverses the file name search. It only moves files over if they will not replace anything.

This switch could be useful, for example, for sending new files to computers in a networked environment. If these computers shared a standard folder structure, you could make a batch script run the same 'replace' command on all of them, and so copy files to them. If any of the computers were switched off or disconnected, and so missed out on the first update, you could run the same script later, and though it would check all computers, it would update only those which needed it. If the files were large, or the network connections slow, this could save a lot of processing time and computer resources, not to mention avoiding the need for manual copying, and tracking which computers were up-to-date.

Replace: updating files
There is also a '/u' switch. U is for 'update'. It only replaces a file in the destination folder if the matched file in the source folder has been modified more recently. So if you open folder two, modify 'file1.txt' and run 'replace /u /p folder1*.txt folder2', then nothing happens: the updated file will not be replaced. If you now modify

140

'file1.txt' in folder one and then run the command, it replaces the out-of-date file in the destination. This is useful, for example, for backing up only files which have changed since they were last backed up. Like the '/a' switch, it allows you to avoid unnecessary copying of files.

Other switches

There are some other switches. If any of your destination files are read-only, they will be protected from being replaced. The '/r' switch overrides that protection. There is also a '/w' switch, which makes the command wait, for the user to insert a disk into their machine, before starting.

Xcopy

What it does: Copies folders, files, or both, overwriting older (less recently modified) files and ignoring empty folders, if directed to. Changes attributes of source or destination files and folders, as directed.

Why use it: to make backups as part of a process, e.g. before the same batch script modifies the original files, or as part of a scheduled backup procedure, e.g. backing up files once a day. To copy batch scripts to a remote computer so they can run locally there. To make dummy copies of folders and files within them, for testing other scripts and code on, before they are deployed on original files elsewhere.

How to use it:

XCopy: introduction

On first sight of the help documentation, the 'xcopy' command might seem overwhelming. It has a large number of switches which modify how it works, in ways both drastic and subtle. It might also seem unnecessary. There is already a 'copy' command, so what more is needed?

To answer briefly: 'copy' is for files; 'xcopy' is for folders and the files within them. This is at least the general focus of the two commands, highlighting their different uses. You can use 'xcopy' to copy folders, so that is a reason to learn about it. Of course, this doesn't make it any easier to get to grips with; there is still a long list of switches to read through. To make it easier, some of the more useful switches are grouped by function below, with examples of how to use them.

The switches introduced here relate to the following areas: the prompt itself, folders and file attributes.

XCopy: prompt switches

The prompt switches are W, P, Y, –Y and Q. Note: although they are referred to by letter here, they still need slashes in front of them in the command line.

W, for 'wait', prompts you to confirm you want to start copying. P prompts you before creating each file in the destination folder. The –Y switch prompts you before copying onto (and thus overwriting) any file, whereas Y stops such prompts. Q, for 'quiet', stops the command window listing files as you copy them. All but W and Q work on a per-file basis.

To try these out, first create two folders. In folder one, create a file and type 'version 1' inside. Run 'xcopy folder1 folder2'. You will see that a copy of the file appears in folder two. Run the command again. Notice how this time it prompts you to confirm that you want to overwrite the last copy you made. Run the command with the Y switch, i.e. 'xcopy /y folder1 folder2'. Note how it no longer prompts you, but does display a list of files copied. Change the text in the original file one to 'version 2'. Run the command with the Q switch as well. Notice how the name of the file copied is now not reported, although the total number of copied files is. If you doubt whether the file has copied correctly, check the copied file contains 'version 2'. Now run the command with the W switch, then the P switch. See what happens.

Note that so far the command has copied files by default. It does not copy the first folder specified, only it contents. To copy folders, you need some more switches.

XCopy: folder switches
The folder switches are S, T, E and I. They can make the command copy the first folder named as a parameter, rather than just its files, into the second.

S copies folders, subfolders and the files inside. T copies folders and subfolders but not the files inside. T is for tree, a term used to describe structures which branch, i.e. the way subfolders branch off from their parent folders. Neither S nor T copies folders without files inside. To do that, you need E. E is for 'Everything'. E copies all folders and subfolders, empty or not, and any files inside. So E includes S in that it copies everything S would, and more. T and E together copy all folders, empty or not, and no files, copying just the directory structure, like an empty shell.

Inside folder one, create a folder called 'subfolder1'. Inside that create a file. Run 'xcopy folder1 folder2'. You will see that the subfolder was not copied into folder two. The command line does not work like Windows Explorer; subfolders are not copied by default. Run the command again, including the S switch this time. Check folder two now and see the difference.

Delete the file from subfolder one, and delete the copied subfolder one from folder two. Run the command again, with the S switch. Once again, the subfolder is not copied, this time because it is empty. Replace the S switch with the E switch and try again. It works, although command prompt may not tell you so in its output. The empty subfolder will appear in folder two.

143

Inside the original subfolder, create two more subfolders and two files. Delete the contents of folder two. Run the command using the T and E switches. Look in folder two and see how the empty folder structure matches the original.

The '/i' switch allows you to name a copied folder by specifying a unique name. It creates the copy whole, as a new folder, rather than overwriting an existing one. It also prevents the system prompting you to say whether you are copying to a file or directory. It pre-selects 'directory' for you.

Run 'xcopy /i folder1 folder3'. You will see the new folder created, and its contents. Delete folder three and run the command without the switch. It will now ask you to confirm that folder three is, in fact, a folder. Do so, and it will work as before. However, this is inconvenient in the command line and worse in a batch file. The switch allows you to avoid this.

You may remember from book one that it is possible to pipe answers to a prompt. In this case, you could run 'echo d| xcopy folder1 folder3' which would make the script answer the prompt when it appears. However, why even have the prompt appear? The '/i' switch is a cleaner solution.

Combined, these switches can do more than just copy whole folders structures and their contents. They can quickly copy a folder structure for use elsewhere, e.g. when setting up a standard set of folders on a company computer. Equally, they can create a tidier copy of the original by excluding empty subfolders.

XCopy: file attribute switches

The file attribute switches are H, R, D, U and EXCLUDE. The next paragraph provides a very brief summary, before the examples start.

H copies hidden and system files. R overwrites read-only files. U, for 'update', only copies a file if there is another with the same name at the destination. It overwrites, but it doesn't add new files to a folder. It's the opposite of '/i'. D for 'date' only copies files modified more recently than the files they are overwriting. With a date parameter, D copies only files changed after that date. EXCLUDE allows you to specify files not to copy, based on their path. If you exclude '.txt', you exclude text files from the copy. If you exclude '\log\', then you exclude files with a folder called 'log' in their path.

To try out the R switch, first set file one in folder two to read-only. If you need to know how to do this, refer to the section on the 'attrib' command. Update the version number in the original file. Run 'xcopy folder1 folder2'. See what happens. Run the command with the R switch and notice the difference. Check the contents of the overwritten file. Check its read-only status: this will be gone.

To try out the H switch, update the version number of file one in folder one, and set the file to hidden; see 'attrib' if needed. Run 'xcopy folder1 folder2'. See how many files get copied. Answer: it's zero, hidden files don't get copied. Run the command with the H switch. This time, it works, and the version number in the file proves it. You may need to unhide your copy to see that though: when the file was copied to the new location, its 'hidden' status was copied too. Before moving on, unhide both the files, so they are available when you run more commands.

The D switch is more suitable for use with files modified on different dates, so doesn't lend itself to the kind of 'instant' examples covered here.

To see the U switch in action, run 'xcopy /u folder1 folder2'. It works. Run 'xcopy /u folder1 folder4'. It prompts you to confirm the folder is a folder, but even if you confirm this, it does not create a new folder. The U switch only allows it to update existing folders. This is useful if, for example, you need to make updates on many systems, but they don't all need every folder. This command would let you update all the folders existing on those systems, without cluttering the file systems with things they don't need.

To see how 'exclude:' works, create a file in 'xcopy1' called 'string.txt', and type '.csv' on the first line. Also, create a CSV file. Run 'xcopy /exclude:string.txt folder1 folder2'. You will see that the CSV file is not copied over. The switch took the string '.csv' from the file named in its parameter ('string.txt') and excluded any files containing that string from the copy operation. If you want to exclude files containing a variety of strings (in the file paths), put each of those strings on separate lines in the 'string' file.

If you have read the rest of the book, you will recognise many of these switches, and their uses, from other commands.

There are even more switches for this command than are covered here. There is also another switch-heavy copy command called 'robocopy'. The copy commands covered here go a long way though, literally, if you use them to copy across a network. Once you read book three, you will know how to connect to the file system of another machine on your network, i.e. map its drives. You will then be able to transfer files between machines. You can even transfer batch files to those other machines and have them run scripts too.

Exercise – back up a folder (backupDir.bat)
Make a script to back up a folder. The backup copy should have the same name, but with '_bak' on the end. Make the script run from command line and take the folder name as a parameter.

The script should delete copy all subfolders, empty or not, and files within the folder.

Volume 3

Introduction

Welcome to Learn Command Line and Batch Scripting Fast, Volume 3! This book is the last of a three part course for people who want to learn how to use command line, write batch scripts, or both. It follows on directly from book two, building on the concepts already covered. It is designed to cover as much as possible, as concisely as possible, with plenty of examples and practice exercises. It uses the same naming system for any dummy files and folders used in the examples.

Naming System

The examples in this book name folders and files in a standard way, to simplify setting them up to practise on.

The system is simple. For each new command, create a folder to practice in. For example, for 'echo', create an 'echo1' folder. Then change directory to that folder. If you create any files inside it, make them text files and name them, 'file1', 'file2', etc, unless otherwise stated. If you create folders there, call them 'folder1', 'folder2', etc. If these folders have subfolders, use 'subfolder1', 'subfolder2', etc.

Command syntax

The syntax, i.e. the switches and parameters, such as file paths, and the order of these, required to use each command is included in the command line help, accessed by typing the command name, followed by '/?'. As such, it is not repeated in this book, which focuses on examples you can try out yourself, explanations of how and why to use the commands, and exercises to practice them. When you do need to check syntax beyond what the examples show, the help provides a ready reference in your command console, so the information doesn't need to be duplicated here.

Navigating networks

This book will examine two ways to navigate networks. You can do both on a home computer. The first way uses Windows Explorer. The second uses just the command line. This chapter will introduce the first way.

Explorer

Although Explorer is a Windows application and not a command, you can still open it by entering its name into the command line. Also, as with other applications opened through command line, you can pass it values in the same way you pass parameters to commands.

For example, running 'explorer %cd%' opens the same folder as your current directory. Running 'explorer C:' opens the C drive. Running 'explorer' with an IP address makes it open the file system of the computer with that IP.

You don't need a network of machines to see how this works. You can try it out with any IP address, including your own.

Run 'ipconfig' and note the IP, or IPv4, address, e.g. '192.168.0.1'.

Run 'explorer \\192.168.0.1\C$', using your own IP in place of the example. This will open Explorer on your C drive. If it doesn't work, try the above, but without the '$'. You can now explore the file system normally. You will see the IP address displayed in the address bar of Explorer as you do, followed by the drive letter, and the folders you enter.

This combination of IP address, drive letter, and any folder/file path is known as a UNC (Universal Naming Convention) path.

Not all commands work across UNC paths directly. If you want a batch script to work with other computers on your network, this presents a problem. The next chapter shows how to solve that problem.

Virtual Drives

When you use the full path name for a folder, including the drive letter and, on a network, the IP address, it quickly becomes very long. Worse, some commands, like 'cd' for example, do not accept UNC paths as parameters. Clearly, this hinders the use of command line over networks.

To get around this, you can map a drive. Mapping a drive means assigning a drive letter to a path, such as a UNC path, making a 'virtual drive'. The computer then treats that drive letter, and therefore the path, like a drive on its own system. This allows commands like 'cd' to use it too. This chapter shows how to do that.

There are several commands for drive mapping. The ones shown here are 'subst', 'pushd', and 'popd'. There is also a 'net use' command, which is effectively a newer version of 'subst'. The three commands above are very simple though, so they are a good way to get started with drive mapping.

Subst

What it does: displays, sets or removes drive letters, i.e. virtual drives, to file paths or UNC paths

Why use it: to allow or support navigation to other computers on a network

How to use it:

Note

The 'subst' command is used here, to introduce drive-mapping, because it is quite basic. There is another drive-mapping command, called 'net use'. This has more features, which you can read about the usual way, by running 'net use /?', if you wish to take drive mapping further. The 'net use' command also works, or performs, in a different way to 'subst'.

Mapping a drive on your own computer

Create a folder 'subst1'. Inside the folder, create another, called 'folder1'. Now navigate to 'subst1' in the command window.

Run 'subst'. This displays a list of any virtual drives you have. There should be none on the list.

Run 'subst Z: %cd%'. This assigns the current folder's path to the virtual 'Z:' drive. Run 'subst' again and you will see this listed.

The '%cd%' in the command gets substituted for the path of the current directory. You could also type out, or paste in, the whole path of the folder. If you were using a UNC path, you would do that. In this case, for local paths, navigating to the folder and using the %cd% environmental variable will save time and typing.

Now run 'Z:' and then 'dir'. You should see 'folder1' inside the Z drive. This is because the Z drive is now another name, or alias, for the much longer path of the 'subst1' folder. The computer acts as if 'subst1' is a real drive, and you can navigate the folders within it as normal, using 'cd', or run other commands within it.

Used locally, within one computer, virtual drives provide a shorthand way to refer to longer paths. Also, they can be used as a kind of path variable, to hold different path depending on the situation. They are not a 'proper' variable, in the sense of being managed by the 'set' command, however.

Drives within drives

Navigate into 'folder1' and assign it to a virtual 'Y:' drive. Run 'subst' to check it worked.

If you have done this from your Z drive, run 'subst' and you will notice that the Y drive is associated with the Z drive plus the folder name. Consider how the Y drive would work if you re-assigned or deleted the Z drive. The short answer is that it wouldn't. So while you can base virtual drives on each other, if you want to, you may find it simpler not to.

Deleting virtual drives

To remove these drives, first run 'C:' to exit them, then run 'subst y: /d' and 'subst z: /d'. As before, check it worked: 'subst' should now output nothing in the command window.

It is good to remove any virtual drives you are no longer using. They outlast the command window and batch scripts, although some actions, like logging out and in again, may clear them. Leaving virtual drives on the system risks other batch scripts or users accessing or modifying their contents by mistake.

Mapping a drive over a network

This follows the same pattern as before, with the addition of the UNC path. The following instructions show how to try it out.

Run 'subst Z:' with your UNC path from earlier, e.g. '\\192.168.0.1\C$'. Run 'explorer Z:' and you will see Explorer open, with the 'virtual drive' name and the same folders as before.

Close Explorer. Run 'Z:' to go to the virtual drive. Run 'dir' to see its contents.

Run 'cd' with any of the folder names. You will see that this works.

Run 'subst /d Z:' to delete your virtual drive.

Uses

Once you have mapped a path, UNC or not, to a drive letter, you can use it in two ways.

You can navigate to that virtual drive. Once within it, you can navigate around it with 'cd', and run commands in and on its folders, and on its files. For example, you can make a folder, delete a file, or copy either. You can copy files and folders to and from your own computer.

You can use the drive as a parameter in your commands. For example, you may enter the drive as the destination parameter in your copy command, and send files to the other computer, without needing to change directory to it.

Exercise – copying across a network (copyToMap.bat)
Create a folder, 'mapFolder'. Create a script to map its UNC path, i.e. including its IP address, to a virtual drive 'Z:'. The script should then copy a file to that virtual drive. It should also clean up after itself at the end, by deleting the virtual drive.

Pushd
What it does: creates a new virtual drive, assigning a file path, or UNC path, to the next available (unassigned) drive letter, counting down from 'Z:' to 'A:'

Why use it: to map networked drives, i.e. on other computers, and navigate to them, and any file paths they have, all in one go.

How to use it:

Note: depending on your system, you may not have access to the 'pushd' command.

Run 'pushd' with your UNC path from earlier, e.g. run 'pushd \\192.168.0.1\C$'. You will see that command prompt has assigned the 'Z:' drive and navigated to it. Run 'dir' to see the folders within your mapped drive.

Repeat the above commands, but add one of your folder names to the 'pushd' parameter, e.g. 'pushd \\192.168.0.1\C$\myFolder'. You will see that the command prompt now assigns the 'Y:' drive, but

154

that the extra folder is included in the path separately, as if you had gone there with 'cd'.

If you run 'pushd' on a local file path, you will see that it does not map a drive at all.

So in summary, for any IP address and drive letter given, 'pushd' maps it to the first available drive letter, counting down from Z. For any folder path given, it acts like 'cd', even if this is given with a drive letter and IP, as in a UNC path. It also navigates to the address parameter automatically. It is like a fast version of 'subst', but only maps actual drives.

This might be useful if you had a variable or unknown number of drives that needed mapping. You could keep assigning drive letters, and the system would choose them for you.

To remove the two virtual drives created with 'pushd', run 'popd' twice.

Popd

What it does: removes the last created virtual drive

Why use it: to remove virtual drives, made with 'pushd', when you have finished using them

Note: again, you may not have this on your system.

How to use it:

When you have finished with a virtual drive created using 'pushd', you can run 'popd'. It removes the last virtual drive you created. So if you have 'Y:' and 'Z:', running it once removes 'Y:', running it again removes 'Z:'.

It is important to remove any virtual drives you are no longer using. They outlast the command window and batch scripts, although a system restart can clear them. Leaving virtual drives on the system risks other batch scripts or users accessing or modifying their contents by mistake.

Subroutines

Scripts can run other scripts. When they do, the scripts they run are called subroutines. There are several ways to have a script run a subroutine, and many good reasons for doing so.

A big advantage of using subroutines is that they help organise code. If a script goes through a certain process several times, the process can be moved to a subroutine. This allows the process to be written once, but called as many times as it is needed, just by running the subroutine. This prevents duplication of lines of code, and so shortens the batch file. Also, if a subroutine needs to be changed, it only needs to be changed in one place. If its code was instead copied into several parts of a script, they would all need to be changed. So subroutines can make scripts easier to maintain.

This way of organising scripts follows the programming concept of modules, where each script is a module designed to do one job, and where the modules can work together, as part of a larger whole. In a modular approach, programs make use of other programs, which do well-defined sub-tasks. They use them many times over, if necessary. In the same way that a bike tyre is designed once, but used in two places, subroutines act as components of a main script.

You can also make a script that you use in lots of other scripts. For example, if you work on a network, and all of your scripts have to map drives, you could make a drive mapping subroutine so that your other scripts can just run that.

To do all this, the command you need is 'call'.

Call

What it does: runs a batch file, or another part of the current batch file, in the same cmd window, without ending the original script

Why use it: to have one script use another

How to use it:

You can use 'call' in several ways. It can run a script file, or another program, and then return control to the current one. It can also run a section of the current script file, and pass it parameters.

Running other scripts and programs

To run another script, first create a batch file 'callMe.bat'. In it, type:

```
@ECHO OFF

HOSTNAME

PAUSE
```

Now create a batch file called 'main.bat'. In it type:

```
@ECHO OFF

CALL callMe

ECHO Finished!

PAUSE
```

Run 'main.bat' now. You will see the hostname. Press any key, to pass the 'pause' prompt, and the word 'Finished' will appear. This shows that the main script ran 'callMe.bat', waited until it finished, and then ran the rest of its own steps.

Now delete 'CALL' from the script, but leave 'callMe' in. Run 'main.bat' again. You will now see only the hostname. With 'call', the main script continues to run when the called script ends; without 'call', it doesn't.

To run, or open, other programs, the same rules apply. To see this, change the script in 'main' so it says 'explorer' instead of 'callMe'. Run it, and the Windows file explorer will open. Again, the parent script will stop after opening the explorer program, unless 'call' is used.

Calling another batch file as a subroutine

If a process is run often in a batch script, or by many batch scripts, it may be worth making that process into a separate file, so that other scripts can use it like a built-in command. The 'call' command allows scripts in other batch files to be used this way, i.e. as subroutines.

For a simple example, suppose all of your scripts back up files to a folder before processing them. You might want to make the backing up part of the script into a subroutine. Here's one way you could do it.

Create a file called 'backup.bat'. In it, type:

    MKDIR backup

    COPY %1 backup

Create a file called 'processFile.bat'. In it, type:

    @ECHO OFF

    CALL backup %1

    ECHO File backed up

    REM the rest of the process would be added here

    PAUSE

Run 'processFile' from the command line, using any file you like as its parameter. It will run 'backup.bat' on that file before continuing.

Exercise – getting an IP address (logMe.bat, callLogMe.bat)

Make a batch file that other batch files can call to log the date and time they ran. It should also log the name of the batch file which called it. In the calling file this is the parameter '%0'. The subroutine should log everything to a new line in a log file, 'log.txt'.

Calling subroutines in the same batch file

You can also use 'call' in a batch file, to run a section of it as a subroutine. You do this by specifying a label in the file as a parameter of 'call', which the script then jumps to. To a very limited extent, you could do this with 'goto', but 'goto' does not pass parameters. The 'call' command can. The following example shows how this works.

Create a batch file 'callSub', and in it type:

```
@ECHO OFF

CALL :%1 %2 %3 %4

EXIT /B

:add

SET /A output = %1 + %2 + %3

ECHO %output%

EXIT /B

:list

ECHO 1) %1

ECHO 2) %2
```

ECHO 3) %3

EXIT /B

Run the script from the command line with 'callSub add 10 20 30'. Now run 'callSub list 10 20 30'. The way the script works is explained below, but if you want to see the command line step through it, comment out '@ECHO OFF' and run your script again.

The script runs the subroutine 'add' or 'list', as the user specifies. To do this, it uses 'call' to jump to a label. This is why the colon ':' is included between 'call' and '%1' in the script: together they form a label name.

The script also passes parameters to its subroutines, using the 'call' command. The values of '%2' to '%4' in the main script are assigned to '%1' to '%3' inside the subroutine. This is because, as far as the command window is concerned, the subroutine under the label is a separate batch script. Therefore, the parameters it takes are assigned to numbered variables, counting from '%1', just as they would be if the script was in a separate file.

After writing its output to the command window, the subroutine ends. The 'exit /b' command only ends the subroutine, not the main script. Once again, the command window treats the subroutine as a separate batch script, so exits from that, not the parent script that called it. Because it was called, it returns control to the main script, which continues from after the 'call' statement. The 'exit /b' command after the 'call' statement then exits the main script, and prevents it continuing on through its own subroutines again.

It is also possible to exit the subroutine using 'goto :eof', i.e. jump to the 'end-of-file label': the end of the batch file. This causes the script to exit the subroutine, as it would exit any batch script upon reaching the end of the file. Equally, reaching the end of its batch file will also cause a subroutine to exit, and return to the point after 'call' statement, so the 'exit /b' on the last line of the program above is actually unnecessary.

Using 'call' in this way allows, and requires, subroutines to be stored in the same batch file but treated as separate scripts.

The advantage of calling subroutines in the same file is that it keeps them together. You could make every module a separate batch file and call those instead. But if your main script had a lot of subroutines, you would end up with a folder full of tiny batch files. This would be inconvenient, especially for uses where you move the batch file to a folder and then run it to process the files there. The call-to-label approach allows you to both organise your code and store it in one file.

Making functions

Suppose you want to make a function: a script that returns a value. You may want to use your function in other batch files, which means they need access to the value it outputs. You may want to use your function in the same file, under a label, in which case the main script needs access to the value it returns.

It is possible to do this by calling the function script from inside a 'for' loop. That technique is covered later. In this section, there is an example of how to do it using 'call' and local variables.

Ideally, the function would set the value of a variable. You could then use the variable in the parent script.

You could do this just by using the functions variable in the script that calls it. Here's a quick example.

Create a file called 'callSquare.bat'. In it, type:

```
@ECHO OFF
```

    SET /P num=Enter a number to square:

    CALL :square %num%

    ECHO %num% squared is %output%.

    EXIT /B

    :square

    SET /A output=%1 * %1

Run 'callSquare' from command line, and enter a number when prompted. It should display the value of the number squared. So far, the script seems to work well.

The problem with variables

Keep the same command window open. Now run 'callSquare' again. This time, don't enter any number when it asks, just press 'enter'. It will now display the value it displayed last time, although this is no longer the correct answer. This is because the 'num' variable remains in the command window, so it is re-used the second time the script runs.

To make your script more reliable, you can make its variables local. You can do this using 'setlocal' and 'endlocal' around the script. Any variables set after 'setlocal' takes effect are cleared by 'endlocal', so they can't be re-used later. To see this, modify 'callSquare.bat' as follows:

    @ECHO OFF

    SETLOCAL

    SET /P num=Enter a number to square:

    CALL :square %num%

    ECHO %num% squared is %output%.

```
ENDLOCAL

EXIT /B

:square

SET /A output=%1 * %1
```

Now open a new command window, so it isn't storing any variables from earlier. Run the script from command line as before, first with a number, then without. You will see that the second time you run the script, it doesn't give any number. Your script is now less error-prone.

The problem with local variables
However, suppose you want to use a function several times within a script. That is, after all, a major reason for using functions in the first place.

Each time it runs, the function sets the same variable: 'output'. Inside the same 'setlocal...endlocal' block, the function variable's value will keep getting overwritten. So if you want to use it later, you need to assign its value to another variable each time. Also, inside the block, you have the same problem with variables as you did before, with 'num'. The 'output' variable can be re-used by mistake too. So you may need to use a 'setlocal...endlocal' block around each use of the 'square' function.

 However, this means that the values the function returns can only be used inside their own blocks. After 'endlocal' has run, the function variable no longer exists. If you assign the value from the function variable into another variable before closing the block, 'endlocal' removes the new variable too.

Beating 'setlocal' and 'endlocal'
To get round this, you can use the following, generic, approach:

ENDLOCAL & SET parentVariable=%childVariable%

With the above method, you can transfer as many values as necessary, by adding extra 'set' commands to the same line, joined by '&'. This works because the command line expands all the variables on each line, before running any of the commands on that line. If you have many variables to set, you can put them on different lines, by putting parentheses '()' at the start and end of the block, as with the 'if' clauses in book one.

It works in three stages. The command line interpreter expands the child script's variables to their values, so the values are written into the line of commands waiting to be run. The 'endlocal' command clears those local variables and resets the command line environment to use global variables, as it did before 'setlocal' took effect. The 'set' command sets those variables from the already expanded values stored in the command text. This leaves the variables ready for use by the parent script.

In summary, the variables are expanded to their values while 'setlocal' still applies, and the values are re-assigned once it does not. If you want to see how it works, run a script containing the above technique, without using '@ECHO OFF'. You will see each of the steps listed.

Passing the parent script's variables to the child is similar. Again, you would combine commands. The fact that 'call' accepts parameters directly makes it even simpler. You can use:

    SETLOCAL & CALL parentVariable

The same principles apply, and it works for the same reasons. To see this in action, modify 'callSquare.bat' to the text below.

    @ECHO OFF

    ENDLOCAL

```
SET /P num=Enter a number to square:

SETLOCAL & CALL :square %num%

ENDLOCAL & SET answer=%output%

ECHO %num% squared is %answer%.

ENDLOCAL

EXIT /B

:square

SET /A output=%1 * %1
```

In the script above, 'output' is the local variable in the function, as before, but it passes its value to 'answer', which is a non-local (global) variable, which the main script can use.

Run the script. It should give the same results as before. Comment out '@ECHO OFF' and run it again. The commands, with their expanded variables, will show how values pass between the main script and the parent.

Variable modifiers

If you run 'call /?' in the command window, and scan through the help for 'call', you will find a section on variable modifiers. These modifiers are a feature which provides a way for batch scripts to read the properties of a file named in the variable. They are not unique to 'call'; you can access them without any special command. To get started with modifiers, follow the example below.

Create a file called 'fileInfo.bat' to contain:

```
@ECHO OFF

ECHO File type is %~x0
```

```
ECHO File size is %~z0 characters

PAUSE
```

Run the script. The '~x' is the extension variable modifier. The '~z' is the file length variable modifier. The '%0' is treated like a parameter variable, but takes it value from the name of the batch file itself. These modifiers give you the batch file's extension, '.bat', and the number of characters it contains.

Exercise – getting information about other files (fileInfo.bat)

A batch file that gets information on itself isn't very useful. A batch file that gets information on any file you choose would be much better.

Change the script to take a file name as a command line parameter, and output that file's details instead of its own. Create a text file to test it on. Then run 'fileInfo file1.txt' and see if it works.

You now have an easy-to-use 'fileInfo' utility. Of course, if you wanted to use it as part of another script, you would need 'call'.

You can extend the information this script provides. To see the full list of variable modifiers available, run 'call /?' and read to the end. There will also be more on variable modifiers in the 'for' command section.

Independent subroutines

There is something else you can do with subroutines, something that 'call' doesn't support. All the scripts so far have run commands one at a time. Even when they run other scripts, they either stop completely, or wait for that script to finish before continuing.

Imagine if your script could run other scripts at the same time. You could have your computer do lots of things at once. With the 'start' command, you can do this.

Start

What it does: runs a program, like Internet Explorer, or a batch script in a new command window

Why use it: to run other batch scripts, at the same time as the main script.

How to use it:

Working in parallel

Suppose you want the command line to display data, and then run commands. Maybe you need screenshots of system information; e.g. hostname, files present, network connection speeds; before you run a process which may, or may fail to, change that information. What would be an efficient way to do this in a batch script?

The script could display the data you need and then continue, and you could go back to screenshot the data afterwards. Of course, if the script outputs a lot of lines, the command window may not scroll back far enough. Also, you have to wait for the script to finish: you could have been saving your screenshot while it ran.

The script could display the data you need, pause to allow you to take a screenshot, and then continue, but this delays the script: running without pause would be better.

The script could write the data it retrieves to a file and then continue, but anyone can write data to a file: a screenshot would be more trusted.

What you need is two command windows: one to display information, one to run a process. Here's how to make a batch script that can run two command windows at once.

Create a batch file called 'getData.bat'. In it, type:

> TITLE %0
>
> HOSTNAME
>
> DIR
>
> PAUSE

This script displays data. Run it to make sure it works. Leave 'echo' on in this batch file, as it shows which commands were used to display the data, making the screenshot better evidence.

Create a batch file called 'doProcess.bat'. In it, type:

> @ECHO OFF
>
> TITLE %0
>
> START getData
>
> ECHO finished>processDone.txt
>
> DIR
>
> PAUSE

Run the script. If you run the script more than once, remember to delete 'processDone.txt' after each time.

This script starts the other in a new window before running its own process, which has been kept short for this example. You can identify which window is from which script by the title text. Note that while 'doProcess.bat' starts the other script before continuing, it does not wait for that script to run all the way through. Both scripts run at the same time. The proof of this is that the 'DIR' command in both windows outputs the same result. This shows that the 'echo' command in 'doProcess.bat' runs and creates the text file before 'getData' finishes, even though 'START getData' comes before 'echo' in the script.

This is important to know, especially if you need data from before any changes are made. It might be worth, for example, building a few seconds delay into the main script, after the start command, to ensure 'getData' has time to finish its job first.

Exercise – delaying tactics (doProcess.bat, getData.bat)
Modify that script. Build in the delay. Compare the results for 'dir' in each command window. They should now be different.

Keeping control
So, the 'start' command lets you run multiple processes at once, and in their own windows, although this can have unpredictable side-effects, as the example above demonstrates. In some situations, you may not be able to predict how long to delay one script while another runs. You might wish to make one script leave a 'message' to the other, to let it know when to continue. For example, a 'goAhead.txt' file in the same directory, which one script could create, and the other script could check for it with 'if exists' every few seconds.

In the example above, a more elegant solution would be to make 'getData' retrieve the data, start 'doProcess', and pause. This simple change would ensure the correct data is obtained and available to view, before the script changes anything.

Exercise – the simple fix (doProcess2.bat, getData2.bat)

Copy the batch files, rename both, and make this change now. Remember to update the script names inside the batch files too, and to delete 'processDone.txt' each time. Run 'getData2.bat' to check it worked.

Exercise – the checkpoint solution (doProcess3.bat, getData3.bat)

If you do want to try the slightly more complex 'goAhead.txt' solution, copy your original files (from before the last exercise), rename them, and try it.

Remember to delete 'goAhead.txt' and 'processDone.txt' between tests. You may even want to make 'doProcess3' start by deleting those text files for you.

For testing purposes, you will need a way to make 'getData' slow down, so that you can see 'doProcess' wait for it to finish before continuing. To do this, you can put in a 'pause' just before the command that creates 'goAhead.txt'.

Other information

There is more to 'start'. Run 'start /?' to see the command switches. Note that this command can also run programs that are not batch script, and run batch script with parameters, if needed.

Checking, and stopping, other programs

If you've ever had trouble closing a program, you may have used Task Manager. This lists the programs currently running on your computer, and provides the means to shut them down if they freeze or otherwise fail to close by themselves.

There are command line equivalents. To view these programs, run 'tasklist'. To stop a program, run 'taskkill' followed by the program name, which you get from 'tasklist'. With these commands, plus 'call' and 'start' for running programs, you can see and control what the computer is doing.

In addition, the command line makes it easy to extend these features. You can, for example, run them on other machines over a network, filter a list of programs, save such lists to a file, or put these commands in a batch script to automate their use.

This chapter will explore all of that, and why you might want to do it.

Tasklist

What it does: lists what processes are running, and details about them, such as which user is running them.

Why use it: to check the above details, and to use them in other commands, e.g. in 'taskkill' to specify which processes to stop.

How to use it:

The basics

Run 'tasklist'. The command window will display a table of processes (programs) that are running on your computer. These include applications, services and scripts. You will see the command window application, cmd.exe. If you have a folder open, you will see explorer.exe and if you have internet explorer running, iexplore.exe.

You will almost certainly have the three applications above, so they will be used in the examples below.

You can change the information 'tasklist' provides: you can request more details, filter the results, or change their format. You can also run the command on a different computer, or with a different set of user permissions, to allow greater or more restricted access.

Extra detail

To request more details, run the command followed by each of these switches, one at a time: M, V, SVC, APPS. For example, 'tasklist /m'. These will give you various technical details about the processes. The switches are defined in the help. Run 'tasklist /?' to see definitions of what they do.

Cutting down

To filter the results, run the command followed by the FI (filter) switch and a criterion enclosed in double quotes. For example, run 'tasklist /fi "imagename eq cmd.exe"'. You will remember that cmd.exe is the command window, which you have open, and you will see that image name is one of the column headers. The 'eq' in the command is short for 'equals'. You have just filtered the list of tasks, so that only those with the name 'cmd.exe' are displayed. Open a second command window and run the same command again. This time you will see two rows in your results, one for each window. They have the same image name, but a different PID (Process ID). PID is therefore a way to distinguish between two processes, in this case, the two windows, of the same application. Knowing the PID allows the user to stop one process without disrupting the other, even for if both programs are from the same application.

173

There are many other filters that can be applied using the same format. For example, 'status' lets you detect if a program is 'not responding'. This is the status of programs that have hung or frozen. A list of these filter names, their possible values, and the operators, like 'eq', that allow them to be compared can be found in the help.

Exercise – using filters (listServices.bat)
Use command line, or make a batch file, to run 'tasklist' and display only the services.

Formatting
To format the results differently, there are yet more switches. Run 'tasklist /nh' to see the process table without headers. Run 'tasklist /fo list' to see the task list in a different format. Run 'tasklist /fo csv' to see the values within each row separated by commas. Now run 'tasklist /fo csv>tasklist.csv' and open the file this creates. It should open in Excel by default. You will see that Excel fits the values into the cells automatically with this format.

Networks
There is also the '/s', or 'system', switch. This allows you to specify an IP address after it, to list processes running on the computer at that address instead of those running on your own machine. This is relevant to networks, allowing you to work across them. There are also switches '/u' for username and '/p' for password, allowing you to run the command as a specified user, if access permissions are an issue.

Exercise – Detective work (getImageName.bat)
Suppose you want to know the image name of a program, e.g. to use in 'taskkill'. How would you do it? One way is to run 'tasklist', open the program, run 'tasklist' again, and compare your two lists until you spot the difference. If you needed to do this a lot, a batch script could speed up your work.

Of course, if you have a shortcut icon to start the program with, you could just look in its properties and get the image name from its 'target' string. You could also track the program file itself down in the file system.

However, you may not always be able to do this. You may need to work on remote computers, where these things are locked down for security, so you can't access them easily. They may have poor network or internet connections, which make some methods of access, like the remote desktop software used in IT support, very slow.

In these cases you need a batch script. But make one to work on your own computer to start with.

Make a script that sends a sorted 'tasklist' to a CSV file, waits while you open a program, then once more sends a sorted 'tasklist', to another CSV. Make it so it waits while you delete the other columns from both CSV files, then compares them with the 'FC' command.

Use this semi-automated method to get the image name for Microsoft Excel. The 'fc' command will list programs from both CSV files, to show where the difference is, which is not needed here. The end result will still be much easier to use than two complete lists.

Taskkill
What it does: stops processes running

Why use it: to stop applications, services or scripts. This allows them to be restarted: a common task in IT support. Programs may be also need to be restarted if their settings have been changed, before those changes can take effect.

How to use it:

175

If you have not already done so, run 'tasklist /?' and have a look at the switches available and what they do. Then run 'taskkill /?' and compare its switches. You will see that most of the switches and options are shared between the two commands.

Whilst the 'tasklist' command tells you which programs are running, the 'taskkill' command stops them running. Both commands allow you to specify a user account and computer to run on. Both allow filters, so you can work with a group of tasks. The 'taskkill' command also allows you to specify image names or PIDs directly with switches, '/im' and '/pid', rather than through filters. This makes it easier to specify a particular process to stop.

In addition, 'taskkill' has a '/t' switch, or 'tree kill'. This terminates not only any specified processes, but also any processes started by them (child processes). This is particularly useful for terminating services. Services, as mentioned before, are programs that run continuously in the background, and may be set to start up automatically. They may often start up other services, or even be designed specifically to manage and ensure the running of those child programs. In such cases, it is necessary to turn off the parent, then the children, so that the parent doesn't detect that the children have stopped and start them up again. The 'tree kill' does that all in one go.

The last switch to note is '/f', for terminating processes 'forcefully', as opposed to 'gracefully'. This is similar to the difference between ending something, e.g. Microsoft Word, in task manager, and clicking the close button in the application itself. The first causes you to get messages, when you open Word again, saying that your files have been recovered. You may even lose some of your unsaved work. The forceful approach may be more reliably effective, but it's a last resort, like pulling the plug to turn off your PC: you would try the power button first.

Open Internet Explorer or Google Chrome. Run 'tasklist' to see the image names for these applications. Run 'taskkill /im iexplore.exe' or 'taskkill /im chrome.exe'. You will see the application windows close. Run 'tasklist' again and you will see the processes are gone.

Open Internet Explorer in two windows, i.e. the one program, Internet Explorer, has two 'instances' running. Run 'tasklist' and repeat the rest of the process in the paragraph above using the '/pid' switch and one of the program's PIDs in place of '/im'. You will see only one of the windows close. This shows how the PID allows you to target instances of programs.

Exercise – Excel yourself (closeExcel.bat)
Open Microsoft Excel. Then, using the image name you found with 'tasklist' and 'fc' earlier, close it again.

Using loops on almost anything

The next section is a big one. It needs to be. It shows how to loop through the file system, a range of numbers and lines of text. But, more than this, it shows how you can use these techniques, with those already covered, to handle almost anything. It will also show just how precisely batch scripts can handle text inside files. Answer: very precisely.

For

What it does: applies code in a loop to folders, files, lines of text in a file, or numbers in a range

Why use it: to apply a process to each member of one of the above groups.

How to use it:

Overview

This command can do a lot. It allows you process sets of items, e.g. file in a folder. Processing items can mean displaying them, applying commands to them, or feeding them to scripts as parameters. The items you can process include lines in a file, files in a folder, subfolders in a folder, or numbers in a range.

With a bit of cunning, you can even use 'for' to loop through an array of variables. The command line does not support an array feature of its own, but you can easily make a fairly close equivalent.

Here is a summary of what 'for' can loop through, and the switches used for each:

No switches: each file in a set of files.

D switch: each folder in a set of folders.

R switch: either of the above, including those in subfolders of the set.

L switch: numbers in a range.

F switch: lines in a file, or in a command output, or text in a string.

This section will introduce these, step by step.

Using 'for' in the command line

Create two files, one text, one CSV, and two folders. Run 'for %i in (*) do echo %i'. You will see each file name in the folder displayed after a new command prompt. If you would prefer a more user-friendly list, without all those command prompts in, run 'echo off' then re-run the 'for' command.

The syntax of this command is as follows:

   FOR variable IN (set) DO command

The variable holds the item which the loop is processing at the time. In this case, the '%i' variable holds each filename in the set, one after the other. The example uses '%i' as its variable name, although anything from '%a' to '%z' would work.

The set defines the list of items the loop should process. In this case, the '*' wildcard defines the set as 'all file names'. This is of course, within the current directory, as per usual.

The command after 'DO' tells the loop what to do with each item. It refers back to the item variable. In this case, the command is 'echo %i', which displays the value stored in the variable, i.e. the filename.

So, what this command says is 'for each file (name) in the current directory, display it'.

Using 'for' in batch script

Make a batch file, call it 'forFiles.bat'. In it, type:

@ECHO OFF

FOR %%i IN (*) DO ECHO %%i

PAUSE

Notice how the 'for' command is almost the same as before. It now has two '%' characters before each variable. In a batch script, 'for' loop variables need the extra '%'. Run the script, and you will see the files listed as before.

Defining your set

Make a copy of your batch file. Call it 'forFiles2.bat'. In the copy, change the set to '(*.txt)', as below.

@ECHO OFF

FOR %%i IN (*.txt) DO ECHO %%i

PAUSE

Run the command and see how it only lists text files. Change the set to '(*.txt *.csv)' to see it list CSV files too. You can list multiple file types, separated by spaces, in your set. You can also list exact filenames, using text without wildcards, or filenames meeting patterns, by combining text and wildcards.

Making changes

The loops so far simply show the contents of their sets. Loops can also process their variables.

Make a copy of 'forFiles2', call it 'forFiles3', and replace 'ECHO %%i' with 'ECHO some text>%%i', as below. As this script does not display text in the command window, you can also cut it down to one line.

    FOR %%i IN (*.txt *.csv) DO ECHO some text>%%i

Run the script and then open your files to see what happened. You should see the line 'some text' in each of the files.

Question: what (unwanted effect) would happen if you used '(*)' as your set in 'forFiles3'?

Answer: You would overwrite your batch script as well.

Exercise – read and write (raw.bat)
Just for practice, can you make the script write each (text and CSV) file's name into that file's own content?

Exercise – make a list (list.bat)
Can you make the script write a list of the files in your folder into a CSV file?

Exercise – one loop, two commands (list2.bat)
Can you make the script write a list of the files in your folder into a CSV file and a text file, all in one line?

Variable modifiers
By default, the 'for' command accesses file names, allowing you to use them in commands. The variable modifiers cause 'for' to access file properties, allowing you to use them in your commands instead. For example, the script below uses the '~x' modifier, which displays the file extension.

    @ECHO OFF

    FOR %%i IN (*) DO ECHO %%~xi

    PAUSE

Type the above script in a file and save as 'property.bat'. Run the file. You will see the extensions of every file in the folder. Change the set to '(file1.txt)'. The loop now gets just the extension of the file you specified. Restricting the set like this makes 'for' access information about a single file: the command does not have to loop.

You can get other information this way. You can get the path with '~p', the drive with '~d', or use '~f' to get the full name: drive, path, name and extension in one string. Other file properties are supported too. Change the '~x' to '~z' and re-run the script to see the file size. If your file has no text in, this may be '0'. Put some text in and run the script again. The size will match the number of characters. If your file has line breaks, these are made up of two characters, and increase the file size accordingly.

Folder switch: /d
Now copy 'forFiles.bat' and rename it 'forFolders.bat'. Add a '/D' switch between 'for' and '%%i'. The new script, should now look like the one below.

```
@ECHO OFF

FOR /D %%i IN (*) DO ECHO %%i

PAUSE
```

Run the script and you will see the folder names listed. The D switch allows you to process folders, instead of files.

Subfolder switch: /r
Make a new file in folder one and a new folder, called 'subfolder', in folder two. Copy 'forFiles.bat' again. Call the copy 'forAllFiles.bat' and add an R switch to its command, as below.

```
@ECHO OFF

FOR /R %%i IN (*) DO ECHO %%i

PAUSE
```

Run the script. Notice how it now also lists the file in the subfolder at the end of its output.

The R switch allows you to loop through the contents of any subfolders too.

Make a copy of 'forFolders.bat', called 'forAllFolders.bat', and add an R switch, as below.

> @ECHO OFF
>
> FOR /D /R %%i IN (*) DO ECHO %%i
>
> PAUSE

Run the script to see all the folders within your current one, including the subfolders. Using the D and R switches together allows you to process folders and their subfolders, i.e. a directory tree.

Number switch: /l
To loop through a range of numbers, use the L switch.

For example, run the command 'for /l %i in (0,1,10) do echo %i'. You will see the numbers from zero to ten displayed.

With this switch, in place of a 'set', there are three values. In the example, zero is the start value, one is the step value, and ten is the end value. The loop displays each value starting from zero, stepping up one at a time, until ten. Change the step value to two and see the difference. You now get multiples of two. Change the start value to five and run again. Run with the values '(10,-1,-10)' and see the result.

You can loop, up or down, through a sequence of numbers, in multiples of your choice. You can use this to process numbers directly, e.g. if your script needs to do calculations. You can also use it to loop through a collection of items not covered by the standard 'for' options. For example, there is no option to loop through computers on a network, but they may have sequential numbers in their IP addresses. What you could do is loop through the IP addresses, applying commands or scripts to each. For example, on a network, you could ping or restart a group of computers this way.

Exercise – make IPs (makeIPs.bat)

Make a script to create the IP addresses 1.2.3.101 to 1.2.3.105, and store them as variables IP101 to IP105. Also, have the script display those variables in the command window afterwards, so you can see it worked.

Arrays

You can also create and work with arrays. The command line does not support arrays directly, but you can mimic them.

Create a batch file 'array.bat' and in it type:

```
@ECHO OFF

FOR /L %%i IN (1,1,10) DO SET /A var%%i=%%i*2

ECHO var1 is %var1%

ECHO var2 is %var2%

ECHO var3 is %var3%

PAUSE
```

Run the script. The loop replaces '%%i' each time, so it runs the command 'set /a var1=1*2', then the command 'set /a var2=2*2', and so on. Each variable up to var10 is now defined and contains a value. Although this array only holds the 'two times table', you could set other items as parts of an array, e.g. the text from lines in a file, the names of files in a folder, etc.

Once items are stored in your array, you can also loop through them with 'for'. To do this, you need to enable delayed expansion and change the command after 'do'. To see an example, make:

@ECHO OFF

FOR /L %%i IN (1,1,10) DO SET /A var%%i=%%i*2

SETLOCAL ENABLEDELAYEDEXPANSION

FOR /L %%i IN (1,1,10) DO ECHO !var%%i!

PAUSE

Run the script again to display your array values.

In the above example, the command line interpreter expands the '%%i' variable, replacing it with numbers, making 'var1', 'var2', etc, before the 'for' command is run. Then, at run-time, the '!var1!', '!var2!', etc, are expanded and replaced with the values in those variables, '2', '4', etc.

Setting variables with delayed expansion

The use of delayed expansion allows 'for' loops to do much more. Specifically, it allows you to set variables and re-use them within 'for' loops. The example below uses this effect to give a running total of the numbers one to five (the mathematical sequence for triangular numbers), but the uses of delayed expansion in loops are not restricted to calculations, or even to numbers.

Create a batch file 'setVars.bat' and in it type:

@ECHO OFF

SET var=0

SETLOCAL ENABLEDELAYEDEXPANSION

FOR /L %%i IN (1,1,5) DO (

        SET /A var=!var! + %%i

        ECHO item: %%i

        ECHO subtotal: !var!

        ECHO.

)

    PAUSE

Run the script. The subtotal is increased by the item value each time, as you would expect. You might also expect to be able to do this with normal expansion. So try swapping the '!' around the variable names for '%'. Run the script again and see what happens.

The '%var%' form always expands to zero, i.e. its value before the loop began. This shows that '%var%' is expanded for all cycles of the loop, before any of them run. This means that normal expansion is useless for processing variables inside 'for' loops. Delayed expansion, however, accesses the value of each variable as each 'DO' command runs. This allows the value of the variable to be both accessed and modified, both within loop cycles and between them.

Exercise – running total (countFiles.bat)
Make a script to list all the files in the current directory, in a numbered list, e.g. 'File1: myFile.txt', 'File2: mySums.csv', and so on, with each item on its own line.

Exercise – stopping part way (top3.bat)
Make a copy of the above script. Change it to run from the command line, and only list the first three files.

Text switch: /f
This switch is used with up to five keywords, which change the way 'for' processes lines of text. These keywords are: 'tokens', 'delims',

'skip', 'eol' and 'usebackq'. The following sections introduce all of them, by way of what they can do.

Getting 'words'

To see how the 'for' command processes, or parses, text in a file, some text is needed. Open your CSV file in notepad, by right-clicking on the file and selecting 'open with' on the context menu. On the first line enter 'l1 v1,l1 v2,l1 v3'. This is short for 'line 1 value 1', etc. Copy the text onto lines two and three and change the line number in the text e.g. 'l2 v1', etc. You now have some dummy text to experiment with. If you open this file with Excel, you will see the comma-separated values form a three-column table.

Create a batch file called 'getWord.bat'. In it type:

@ECHO OFF

FOR /F %%i IN (file2.csv) DO ECHO %%i

PAUSE

Run the script. This script displays the text of each line, up to the first space or tab. If the file was made up of words, i.e. plain text, this might be useful. As the CSV file stores table values, it isn't so useful here. To change how the command extracts the text, and so make it more useful, some parameters are needed.

Getting columns

Create a batch file called 'getColumn.bat'. In it type:

@ECHO OFF

FOR /F "delims=," %%i IN (file2.csv) DO ECHO %%i

PAUSE

Run the script. Notice how the result contains only values from the first 'column'. By setting the 'delims' (delimiters) value to be a comma, the script now splits each line on the commas, instead of on the default character: spaces.

This allows access to the first 'column' stored in a CSV file. To access the other columns, you need another parameter: 'tokens'.

Edit 'getColumn.bat' to read as below:

```
@ECHO OFF
FOR /F "tokens=2 delims=," %%i IN (file2.csv) DO ECHO %%i
PAUSE
```

Run the script. It will display the second column's values. By default, 'for' takes the first part of each line. By using 'tokens', you can specify that you want other parts.

The 'delims' character is the one used to split each line of text into sections. The number after 'tokens' says which of those sections to use.

Exercise – using tokens (getColumn3.bat)
Copy the script and change it to make it display only the third column of the CSV file.

Getting lines
You may want a line, or lines, of text, rather than a column. You may also want complete lines, not just a word or a section.

Create a file 'getLines.bat' and in it type:

```
@ECHO OFF
FOR /F "tokens=*" %%i IN (file2.csv) DO ECHO %%i
PAUSE
```

Run the script. Having 'tokens=*' in your loop makes it output each line in full.

Change the script to read:

@ECHO OFF

FOR /F "tokens=* skip=1" %%i IN (file2.csv) DO ECHO %%i

PAUSE

Run the script now. It will skip line one from the file and just display the others. Change the script so that 'skip=2' and then run it again. It skips lines one and two and displays line three only. By using 'skip', you can exclude unneeded lines from the start of the file.

Of course, you may want to exclude lines from the end of the file too. You may want just one line from a thousand line file. You may need only the lines twelve to fifteen. In these situations, it would be useful to have a 'skip' option for the lines after a specified line number. This would allow you to retrieve the exact lines you need, saving you from having to read and process extra lines in your script. It would save a huge amount of running time in cases where information had to be retrieved from large files, or over networks.

The command does not provide an option to do that, but this book will show you how to do it anyway.

Exercise – one-liners (get1Line.bat)

Copy 'getLines.bat' and rename it 'get1Line.bat'. Change the new script file to skip line one of 'file2.csv' output the second line and then stop. You will need to have the script jump out of the loop part way through. Try out a few ways before looking at the answer.

Exercise – better one-liners (getLineNum.bat)

Change the script so you specify which line you wish to retrieve, when running it from the command prompt. Test it for lines two and three.

Exercise – even better one-liners (getAnyLineNum.bat)

Try to get line one of your CSV file using your script. If it doesn't work, change the script to make it work for that line too.

Exercise – find a value (getValue.bat)

Make the script take a second parameter. With this parameter, the user should be able to specify which column they want. The finished script should allow them to pull a value from any row and column in the file.

With a bit more work, your script can get any number of lines, columns, or values. You can do this by included a variable in the 'for' loop to count up to a certain number of lines, and then exit the loop. For this, you would need delayed expansion, as covered earlier. You could also use the script as a subroutine, calling it repeatedly from another script, with different parameters each time.

Multiple columns

Suppose you need to get more than one piece of each line. You can also use the 'tokens' value to do this. Copy 'getColumn.bat', save it as 'get2Columns.bat' and edit it to read:

```
@ECHO OFF

FOR /F "tokens=1,2 delims=," %%i IN (file2.csv) DO ECHO %%i and %%j

PAUSE
```

Run the script. The first two columns are now displayed. The second variable '%%j' holds the second value from the line. The

'%%j' variable is assigned to the second token specified in the first part of the 'for' command. It is assigned automatically, being the next letter after 'i' in the alphabet. If you put '%%a' in the first part of 'for', token two gets assigned to a '%%b' variable.

It is also possible to specify a range of tokens, i.e. 'tokens=1-3'. Try it. Copy 'get2Columns.bat' to make 'get3Columns.bat' and change the tokens to this. Then change the 'DO' section to 'ECHO %%i and %%j and %%k'. Run the script to see all three sets of column values displayed.

Exercise – re-using those variables (reverse.bat)
Make the script display the column values in reverse order.

Exercise – turn the tables (columnSwap.bat)
The example above might seem trivial, but it's not. If you can re-order the columns in the command window, you can re-order them in the file.

A simple way to do this is to send the 'for' loop's output to a temporary file, use that file to overwrite your original, and then delete the temporary one. Try to make a script to do this. You may wish to make a copy of your CSV file before you start. This will save re-typing it, if it gets overwritten incorrectly.

Test your script. When you have it working, run it again, to put your columns back in the right order.

Implications
It follows from this, that you can also delete columns in the file, by overwriting it with only some of its own columns. You can even add columns, by sending extra text to your temporary file from inside the 'for' loop.

The techniques, already covered, for skipping lines, counting items in a loop, and leaving loops early combine to allow you to do similar things with lines of text, or rows in a table.

Together, all of this gives you a powerful and precise way to both get and set values in a CSV file. Indeed, it provides ways to work with text in any text-based (i.e. non-binary) file.

Variable numbers of columns

Suppose you want to select a group of columns, words, or similar; but you don't know how many you will need. Maybe you want to make a batch script that allows the user to select all tokens after a specified token number. You can do this by putting '*' after that number, i.e. to get the second column and then everything after it, use 'tokens=2,*'.

Copy 'get2Columns.bat' and edit it to contain:

```
@ECHO OFF

FOR /F "tokens=1,* delims=," %%i IN (file2.csv) DO ECHO %%i and %%j

PAUSE
```

Run the script above. It shows the first column's values, the word 'and', then, as one string, the next two columns' values. Change the script to use 'tokens=2,*', and run it again. It outputs the values from column two, the word 'and', and then the values from column three.

Comment characters

Open 'file1.txt' and, in it, type:

```
Some code

;some comment
```

Some code then; some comment

Create a batch file 'justCode.bat' and in it type:

@ECHO OFF

FOR /F "tokens=* eol=;" %%i IN (file1.txt) DO ECHO %%i

PAUSE

The 'eol' stands for 'End Of Line' character. Run the batch file. You may expect to see only the code, but in fact it does show our 'comment' text at the end of line three. The 'eol' parameter allows the loop to skip past, i.e. exclude, lines which start with the character specified. It does not affect lines which only contain the 'eol' character, but don't start with it.

Often, program files contain lines of notes in plain English. While batch script marks these comments out with 'REM' or '::', many programming languages have a comment character. These are used at the start of lines, to tell the computer not to try to run those lines as code.

By using 'eol', you can, for example, extract from a program's file all the lines the programmer did not mark as comments, i.e. all the code. Of course, some languages, like JavaScript, allow multi-line comments, which would not be skipped. Others, like VBA and VB Script, use single-line comments, marked with apostrophes at the beginning, so 'eol' can be used.

Usebackq – File names with spaces in
Create a text file called 'myFile3.txt' and type some text in it.
Create a batch script called 'allText', containing the following code:

@ECHO OFF

FOR /F "tokens=*" %%i IN (myFile3.txt) DO ECHO %%i

PAUSE

Run the script and you will see the file contents. Now put a space between 'myFile' and '3' in both the file name and the script. Run the script again and see what happens. The error message will confirm that the command is now looking for a file called 'myFile'. Of course, this file does not exist. The command reads the text between the brackets as a file name, but when it finds the space, it assumes that is the end of the name, and that any text after the space is a new name. This allows it to process multiple files in one loop, but, in this case, it breaks the command.

Update the script with 'usebackq' and put double quotes around the file name, as follows:

@ECHO OFF

FOR /F "usebackq tokens=*" %%i IN ("myFile 3.txt") DO ECHO %%i

PAUSE

Run the script again. Now it works. By using 'usebackq', you change the way the command treats quotes after 'IN'.

Looping through strings

Rather than looping through the text of a file, you can use strings directly, as in:

@ECHO OFF

FOR /F "tokens=2" %%i IN ("I am a string") DO ECHO %%i

PAUSE

This script gets the second word, 'am'. In a real script, you would probably put a variable in place of "I am a string", but this example shows the syntax. Note that it uses double quotes, but not 'usebackq'. The double quotes mark out string, but only with 'usebackq' would the string be taken as a file name.

This does leave the problem: what if the string contains double quotes anyway?

Once again, you need 'usebackq', as in this script:

```
@ECHO OFF

FOR /F "usebackq tokens=2" %%i IN ('I "am" a string') DO ECHO %%i

PAUSE
```

This script displays the second word, including the double quotes around it. By using 'usebackq' you switched the command to take single-quoted text as a string input.

Of course, this leaves the problem: what if the string contains single quotes anyway?

The answer is to go back to what you had before: double quotes around the string, and no 'usebackq' keyword.

Looping through command output

You can also loop through the output of commands, like 'systeminfo'. You will need to put the command name in single quotes. For example, the following script will loop through and output all of the 'ipconfig' command's text.

```
@ECHO OFF

FOR /F "tokens=*" %%i IN ('ipconfig') DO ECHO %%i

PAUSE
```

Setting variables from text

You can now loop through both command output and file contents, with each line of text already stored, temporarily, in a variable: '%%i'. This is a short step from using commands, or file text, to set variables that you can then re-use in your script. The example below shows one way this can be made to work.

Create a batch file, 'getIP.bat'. In it, type:

```
@echo off

FOR /F "tokens=*" %%I IN ('getIPLine') DO SET IP=%%I

ECHO IP = %IP%

PAUSE
```

Create another batch file, 'getIPLine.bat'. In it, type:

```
IPCONFIG | FIND "IPv4 Address"
```

The exact text you need 'find' to search for may vary with your system. You can check what it should look for by running 'ipconfig' yourself. Run 'getIPLine' from the command line first, to test it. It should return only one line, the line containing the IP address of your computer.

Now run 'getIP'. You will see that it outputs the value of the '%IP%' variable, which has outlasted the 'FOR' loop. To get just the IP out of the line would require a little more work, using your string processing skills. However, the point is proven: you can set variables from command output, you just need to use a 'FOR' loop to do it.

Loops, pipes, and subroutines

This exercise will cover using piped input in a batch script. It will also prepare you to perform 'find and replace' operations on files automatically. Here's how to do it.

First, run the command 'systeminfo> sysInfo.txt'. This will give you a data file to work with.

Second, make a batch file called 'mainReplace.bat'. In it, type:

@echo off

FOR /F "tokens=*" %%I IN (sysInfo.txt) DO ECHO %%I | CALL lineReplace

PAUSE

This script will send (pipe) each line of text from the file to the 'lineReplace' script.

Third, make a batch file 'lineReplace.bat'. In in, type:

@echo off

SET /P string=%*

ECHO %string%

This script will run once per line of text. It will accept each line of text as '%*' and assign it to the 'string' variable. It uses the P switch to do this, because piped input is STDIN, the same as user input. Then it displays the contents of the variable, unchanged, to show everything works so far.

Exercise – find and replace, a primer (lineReplace1.bat)
Modify 'lineReplace.bat' to process the text it receives. For example, have it replace 'Microsoft' with 'Apple' when it writes to the command window. If you change the name of the file, as above, remember to update the file name that your other batch script calls too.

197

Exercise – find and replace, the real deal (mainReplace2.bat, lineReplace2.bat)
Modify the scripts, so that they change the text in 'sysInfo.txt' itself.

Dealing with unknown numbers of parameters

Files can contain any number of lines. Folders can contain any number of files. In cases like these, you have the 'for' loop to help. But there is one more unpredictable quantity in batch scripting. Suppose you need to design a script to accept a list of filenames as parameters. The user can enter any number of parameters. To cope with this, you need the 'shift' command.

Shift

What it does: moves parameter values to the preceding parameter, i.e. the value in variable %1 is overwritten by the value in %2. The value in %2 is replaced by the one in %3, and so on.

Why use it: to allow a batch script to process a large, variable, or unknown number of parameters

How to use it:

Using parameters

The shift command acts on parameters. Although parameters have been used a lot in this course already, there is a little more to cover about them before moving onto the command itself.

When running a command, you can often use switches and parameters to modify how it works and what it works on.

When running a batch script from the command line, you can do the same thing. Batch scripts have built-in parameter variables to hold values entered after the script name. These variables can be used within the script.

The zero parameter

The first variable, '%0', holds the file name itself, the name of the batch script being called. This works differently when you run the script from command line than it does when running it from

Windows Explorer. To see the effect, create a batch file 'get0' and in it, type:

> @ECHO OFF
>
> ECHO Parameter zero is: %0
>
> PAUSE

Run 'get0' from Explorer and the command line. Notice the difference. One displays the full path, in quotes; the other displays just the batch file name.

Exercise – unintended consequences

Suppose you decide you want the '>' character to appear in your batch script results, to make it look more like a command prompt. Make the second batch file line read as below:

> ECHO Parameter zero is:>%0

Run the batch file, and then open it. Can you work out what happened?

The answer is included in the next exercise.

Exercise – escape the consequences (get0.bat)

Can you fix the batch script above, so it works as intended?

The other parameters

The other parameters are '%1' to '%9' and are based on the order in which they follow the script name. For example, if you write a script file 'myCommand.bat' and run 'myCommand File1.txt File2.txt', then each file name is passed as a parameter to the batch script. To use the values of those parameters in your script, you would refer to '%1' and '%2' respectively. So the line 'type %1' in the script would display the contents of 'File1.txt' in the command window.

These parameter variables continue up to '%9'. If you want your script to use more parameters after that, or take an unknown number of parameters, you need to use 'shift'. Read on to see how.

Using 'shift'

The 'shift' command moves parameter values down through the parameters. So, in the example above, the line 'shift' moves 'file2.txt' into '%1' and 'file1.txt' into '%0'. The value that was stored in '%0' is lost.

To see how shift works, create a file, 'myShift.bat', and in it type:

```
@ECHO OFF

ECHO The variable values are %0, %1, and %2

PAUSE

SHIFT

ECHO The variable values are now %0, %1, and %2

PAUSE
```

Run 'myShift 1 2'. You will see how the values shift leftwards in the line. Notice also that, after the shift, the value of '%2' is gone. Because there was no '%3' value, the variable '%2' is now an empty string, so there is nothing to appear in its place.

If there are more than nine parameters after the script name, the usefulness of 'shift' becomes clearer. Using 'shift' the tenth of those parameters is moved into '%9' and becomes available for processing. If there are more parameters, a loop can be used to keep shifting until there are no parameters left, i.e. until '%9' is an empty string. This allows the script to cycle through the extra parameters, storing each in '%9'. While stored there, they can be either used directly, or copied into other variables and saved for later use.

Switch usage

Shift has a '/n' switch, where the 'n' is replaced with the variable number to start shifting parameters into. For example, 'shift /2' ignores '%0' and '%1', but moves the value of '%3' into '%2'. To see the '/n' switch in action, add it to the above batch file and run 'myShift 1 2 3'.

Note that the highest value you can use as 'n' is 8.

Exercise – minimal effort (easyShifter.bat)

Make a script which takes parameters one to seven, and keeps them to use directly, but shifts parameters eight to ten through '%8', saving them into named variables, i.e. 'var8', 'var9', 'var10', for later use. Have the script display the variables, and the first seven parameters, at the end, to show that they are stored correctly and ready for further use.

Exercise – doing a better job of it (shifter.bat)

Make a script which takes parameters one to seven, and keeps them to use directly, but shifts any higher parameters through '%8', saving them into named variables, e.g. 'var8', 'var9', 'var10', etc, for later use. Have the script display the variables, and the first seven parameters, at the end, to show that they are stored correctly and ready for further use. Make the script able to cope with an unknown number of variables.

The everything parameter

Finally, there is a '%*' parameter. This is the whole set of parameters, excluding the script name, taken all together. To see how this works create a batch file, 'asterisk.bat', and in it type:

```
@ECHO OFF
```

```
ECHO %*

PAUSE
```

Run 'asterisk 1 2 3 4 5 6 7 8 9 10 11 12' to see the result.

This allows your batch script to pick up as many parameters as you like, and you don't even need 'shift' to do it. However, it treats them like one parameter. This would still be useful in some cases. If you wanted to log which parameters the command had been run with, for example, it would be far easier to send the whole parameter string to a log file at once.

Exercise – log everything (asterisk.bat)
Change the script to run from command line, and log the command string that ran it (or rather, a very close copy of that string) to a text file.

Conclusion - where to go from here

You are now familiar with the command line. You know how to use many of its commands. You can combine and automate these into batch scripts.

Command line can do much more. There are many more specialised areas of Windows system administration. These have commands too. Sometimes they have their own command-line tools, where different commands apply. Sometimes there are extensions you can add to your command line, to give it extra commands. Here's a selection of those areas, and some tools and commands you might like to read up on.

Warning
The commands and tools below change or affect your computer system(s). As such, it is advisable to research them, before running any of them. Otherwise, you risk, among other things, losing data or damaging Windows so that it will not load up.

Installing programs
The 'MsiExec' command allows you to install, and uninstall, programs.

Managing Windows systems
The 'WMIC', or 'Windows Management Instrumentation Command-line', allows you to get and set Windows system data. It also allows you to do these things across a network. If you want to find out how many processors your computer has, or the screen height in pixels, for example, you can use WMIC to find out. If you want a remote machine to have a different hostname to its current one, you can use WMIC to change it.

PSTools

This is the answer to the question 'How do I get another computer to do that?' PSTools is a set of commands for working across a network. It allows you to make remote computers run commands locally. This is different from how commands normally work. Normally, if you run a command from your computer, your computer processes it, even if that command affects another computer across the network. With PSTools commands, such as 'psexec', your computer gets remote computers to process the commands themselves. It also brings any output back to your machine's command window.

There are commands, like 'hostname' or 'chkdsk', which only run locally. You cannot, for example, pass an IP address to 'chkdsk' and have it fix another PC's hard disk. However, you can use 'psexec' to make a remote computer run 'chkdsk' on itself.

PSTools is an extension to the normal command line, so must be installed before you can use any of its commands. You can download PSTools from Microsoft.

Managing disks

There are various commands for this. There is also the 'diskpart' utility, which runs from command line and includes its own set of disk management commands.

Managing services

If you want to turn services on or off, or set them to start automatically when Windows loads up, you can do that, for both local and remote computers. Look into the 'sc' (service centre) and 'net' commands, e.g. 'sc config', 'net start', 'net stop', etc.

Net commands

There are many 'net' commands, aside from the two above, to interact with remote computers. They are not limited to managing services.

More commands

This by no means covers all the things the command line can do. You can find further resources online, such as Microsoft's TechNet website, which provides an A-Z list of commands. Many of these, like 'diskpart', are really utilities with multiple commands of their own. Many others are networking commands. Whatever you do, the concepts of command line and automation covered in this book should make it that much easier to succeed at. I hope this course helped you on your way.

Author's Note

If you found this book useful, please let others know by leaving a review on its Amazon page.

If you feel this book could be improved in some way, let me know on the email below.

authordarmstrong@gmail.com

Thank you for reading.

D Armstrong

March 2015

You've finished. Before you go...

More by this author

SQL: Learn SQL Fast, by D Armstrong

Excel: Learn Formulas Fast, by D Armstrong

Learn VBA Fast, Volume I by D Armstrong

Learn VBA Fast, Volume II by D Armstrong

Learn VBA Fast, Volume III by D Armstrong

Keyboard Wizard by D Armstrong

IT Support, an A-Z Guide by D Armstrong

Answers – Volume 1

absA.bat
@echo off

SET /A output = %1 - %2

IF %output% LSS 0 SET /A output *= -1

ECHO %output%

absB.bat
@echo off

IF %1 GTR %2 (

    SET /A output = %1 - %2

) ELSE (

    SET /A output = %2 - %1

)

ECHO %output%

backup.bat
@echo off

TYPE %1.txt>%1.bak

char3.bat
@echo off

SET string=%1

ECHO %string:~2,1%

clearFile.bat
@echo off

echo.>file1.txt

Colour Codes
Color 17

custom.bat
COLOR 0A

TITLE Command Testing

CLS

custom2.bat
CD C:\(your file path here)\Batch

CLS

divideA.bat
@echo off

SET /A output = %1 / %2

ECHO %output%

divideB.bat
@echo off

IF %2==0 (

    SET output=Infinity

) ELSE (

    SET /A output = %1 / %2

)

ECHO %output%

flush.bat
@echo off

ECHO.>chat.txt

gather.bat
@echo off

VER>>gather.txt

VOL>>gather.txt

HOSTNAME>>gather.txt

getIP.bat
@echo off

REM get device number

SET /P num=enter device number:

REM calculate 3rd IP number

SET /A IP3 = num / 256

REM calculate 4th IP number

SET /A IP4 = num %% 256

REM output complete IP address

ECHO 1.2.%IP3%.%IP4%

PAUSE

info.bat
```
@echo off

ECHO The Information Interface

ECHO.

ECHO Options:

ECHO 1 - Display version of Windows

ECHO 2 - Display volume details

ECHO 3 - Display name of host device

ECHO.

SET /p input=Enter a number from 1 to 3 and press enter:

IF %input%==1 VER

IF %input%==2 VOL

IF %input%==3 HOSTNAME

PAUSE
```

info2.bat
```
@echo off

ECHO The Information Interface

ECHO.

ECHO Options:

ECHO 1 - Display version of Windows

ECHO 2 - Display volume details
```

ECHO 3 - Display name of host device

ECHO.

:choose

SET /p input=Enter a number from 1 to 3 and press enter:

IF NOT "%input:~1%"=="" ECHO Too many characters entered! & GOTO choose

IF %input% GTR 3 ECHO Too high! & GOTO choose

IF %input% LSS 1 ECHO Too low! & GOTO choose

IF %input%==1 VER

IF %input%==2 VOL

IF %input%==3 HOSTNAME

PAUSE

isHere.bat
@echo off

IF EXIST %1 (ECHO file found) ELSE ECHO file not found

left10.bat
@echo off

SET string=%1

ECHO %string:~0,10%

logErr.bat

```
@echo off

SET /p input=Enter command to log errors for:

REM run command and save its error text in a temporary file

%input% 2>tempErrLog.txt

IF %errorlevel%==0 (

    ECHO No error logged

) ELSE (

    REM copy the command and its result to a permanent log file

    ECHO At %time%, the command "%input%" returned:>>logErr.txt

    TYPE tempErrLog.txt>>logErr.txt

    REM add blank lines to separate entries

    ECHO.>>logErr.txt

    ECHO.>>logErr.txt

    ECHO error log updated

)

REM delete the temporary file's contents

ECHO.>tempErrlog.txt

PAUSE
```

logIn.bat
@echo off

SET /p input=Enter text to add to log file:

ECHO At %time% on %date%, %username% logged: %input%>>log.txt

ECHO log updated

logOut.bat
@echo off

SET /p input=Enter command to log results for:

ECHO The command "%input%" returned:>>logOut.txt

ECHO.>>logOut.txt

%input%>>logOut.txt

ECHO.>>logOut.txt

ECHO log updated

PAUSE

mod.bat
@echo off

SET /A output = %1 %% 5

ECHO %output%

reader.bat
@echo off

:start

    CLS

TYPE chat.txt

TIMEOUT 3 > nul

GOTO start

right10.bat
@echo off

SET string=%1

ECHO %string:~-10%

square.bat
@echo off

SET /A output = %1 * %1

ECHO %output%

sysInfo.bat
@echo off

SYSTEMINFO>sysInfo.txt

trim.bat
@echo off

SET string=%1

ECHO %string:. =. %

twoLines.bat
@echo off

ECHO. & ECHO.

UKtoUS.bat
@echo off

SET /P string=<ebook.txt

SET string=%string:focussed=focused%

SET string=%string:maths=math%

ECHO %string%>ebook.txt

PAUSE

writer.bat
@echo off

COLOR 0D

:start

    SET /P msg=Enter your message:

    ECHO %username% says: %msg%>>chat.txt

GOTO start

writer2.bat
@echo off

COLOR 0D

:start

    SET /P msg=Enter your message:

    ECHO %username% says: %msg:&=^&%>>chat.txt

GOTO start

Your Version
Prompt vg$s

Answers — Volume 2

backup.bat
@ECHO OFF

COPY *.txt *.bak

backupDir.bat
@ECHO OFF

XCOPY /s /e /i %1 %1_bak

beginning.bat
@ECHO OFF

FINDSTR "^2" test.txt

PAUSE

bootTime.bat
SYSTEMINFO| FIND /I "boot time"

checkInput.bat
@ECHO OFF

:begin

    SET /P input=Enter a variable:

IF NOT DEFINED input GOTO begin

ECHO You entered %input%

PAUSE

clearAll.bat
ATTRIB -r -h /D /S

218

commas.bat
```
@ECHO OFF

FINDSTR "1,*000" test.txt

PAUSE
```

endIn1Digit.bat
```
@ECHO OFF

FINDSTR "[^0-9][0-9]$" test.txt

PAUSE
```

endInDigit.bat
```
@ECHO OFF

FINDSTR "[0-9]$" test.txt

PAUSE
```

ending.bat
```
@ECHO OFF

FINDSTR "1$" test.txt

PAUSE
```

getCSVs.bat
```
@ECHO OFF

FINDSTR "\.csv" test.txt

PAUSE
```

justOS.bat
```
@ECHO OFF

SYSTEMINFO| FINDSTR /B OS
```

labelsOnly.bat
@ECHO OFF

::this is a comment, a label is on the line below

:label1

REM this is a comment too, a label is on the line below

:label2

FINDSTR "^:[^:]" labelsOnly.bat

PAUSE

makeDummy.bat
@ECHO OFF

REM Present user with options

:begin

    ECHO Dummy file generator

    ECHO.

    ECHO Choose a file type. Enter:

    ECHO 1 for .txt

    ECHO 2 for .csv

    ECHO 3 for .html

    SET /P fileType=Type?

    REM Make time variable

```
SET timeMade=%time::=%

SET timeMade=%timeMade:.=%


REM Choose dummy file type, and make it

GOTO case%fileType%

:case1

        ECHO.>file%timeMade%.txt

        GOTO begin

:case2

        ECHO.>file%timeMade%.csv

        GOTO begin

:case3

        ECHO.>file%timeMade%.html

        GOTO begin
```

makeDummy2.bat
```
@ECHO OFF

SETLOCAL ENABLEDELAYEDEXPANSION

REM Define file type variables

SET fileType1=txt

SET fileType2=csv

SET fileType3=html
```

REM Present options to user

:begin

    ECHO Dummy file generator

    ECHO.

    ECHO Choose a file type. Enter:

    ECHO 1 for %fileType1%

    ECHO 2 for %fileType2%

    ECHO 3 for %fileType3%

    SET /P num=Type?

    REM generate time variable

    SET timeMade=%time::=%

    SET timeMade=%timeMade:.=%

    ECHO.>file%timeMade%.!fileType%num%!

GOTO begin

mismatchTotal.bat
@ECHO OFF

FIND /I /V /C "%1" %2

mkdirs.bat
@ECHO OFF

```
SET /P setup=Press 'S' to create side-by-side, or 'W' to create within each other

GOTO Case%setup%

    :CaseS

        MKDIR %1

        MKDIR %2

        MKDIR %3

        EXIT /B

    :CaseW

        MKDIR %1\%2\%3
```

myCopy.bat
```
COPY file1.txt folder1\NewName.txt
```

parent.bat
```
@ECHO OFF

ECHO Attempting to restore file %1.txt

CALL safeRestore %1

GOTO Case%errorlevel%

    :Case0

        ECHO File restored

        EXIT /B

    :Case1
```

ECHO There is no backup file to restore from

restore.bat
@ECHO OFF

DEL %1.txt

REN %1.bak %1.txt

restoreAll.bat
@ECHO OFF

DEL *.txt

REN *.bak *.txt

restoreDir.bat
@ECHO OFF

RMDIR /S /Q %1

MOVE %1_bak %1

safeRestore.bat
@ECHO OFF

IF EXIST %1.bak (DEL %1.txt) ELSE EXIT /B 1

REN %1.bak %1.txt

safeRestoreAll.bat
@ECHO OFF

COPY /Y *.bak *.txt

DEL *.bak

scanLogs.bat
@ECHO OFF

MORE log*.txt

PAUSE

sortFile.bat
@ECHO OFF

SORT %1.txt /O %1.txt

sortFileR.bat
@ECHO OFF

SORT %1.txt /R /O %1.txt

stringReplace.bat
@ECHO OFF

SET string=%3

SETLOCAL ENABLEDELAYEDEXPANSION

ECHO !string:%1=%2!

trickyEnd.bat
@ECHO OFF

FINDSTR /r /c:" .$" test.txt

PAUSE

twoWords.bat
@ECHO OFF

FINDSTR "alert.*error" test.txt

PAUSE

zipCode.bat
```
@ECHO OFF

FINDSTR "^[0-9][0-9][0-9][0-9][0-9]$" test.txt

PAUSE
```

Answers – Volume 3

asterisk.bat
```
ECHO %0 %*>>log.txt
```

callLogMe.bat
```
@echo off

CALL logMe %0

REM If this was not just a test script...

REM ...the rest of the script would go here.

ECHO Script completed!

PAUSE
```

closeExcel.bat
```
@echo off

TASKKILL /IM excel.exe

PAUSE
```

columnSwap.bat
```
FOR /F "tokens=1-3 delims=," %%i IN (file2.csv) DO ECHO %%k,%%j,%%i>> file3.csv

TYPE file3.csv> file2.csv

DEL file3.csv
```

copyToMap.bat
```
@echo off

SUBST Z: \\(your IP address here)\(your folder path here)\mapFolder
```

REM IP address checked with 'IPCONFIG'

REM Folder path copied in from Windows Explorer

REM ':' after drive letter replaced with '$'

COPY file1.txt Z:

SUBST /D Z:

countFiles.bat
```
@ECHO OFF

SET count=0

SETLOCAL ENABLEDELAYEDEXPANSION

FOR %%i IN (*) DO (

        SET /A count=!count! + 1

        ECHO File!count!: %%i

)
PAUSE
```

doProcess.bat
```
@ECHO OFF

TITLE %0

START getData

TIMEOUT /T 3

ECHO finished>processDone.txt

DIR

PAUSE
```

doProcess2.bat

```
@ECHO OFF

TITLE %0

ECHO finished>processDone.txt

DIR

PAUSE
```

doProcess3.bat

```
@ECHO OFF

TITLE %0

DEL processDone.txt

DEL goAhead.txt

START getData3


:startLoop

        TIMEOUT /T 3

IF NOT EXIST goAhead.txt GOTO startLoop


ECHO finished>processDone.txt

DIR

PAUSE
```

easyShifter.bat

```
@echo off
```

```
SET var8=%8

SHIFT /8

SET var9=%8

SHIFT /8

SET var10=%8

ECHO The first 7 parameters are: %1 %2 %3 %4 %5 %6 %7

ECHO var8=%var8%

ECHO var9=%var9%

ECHO var10=%var10%

PAUSE
```

fileInfo.bat
```
@echo off

ECHO %~x1

ECHO %~z1

PAUSE
```

get0.bat
```
@ECHO OFF

ECHO Parameter zero is:^> %0
```

REM '^' escapes '>', preventing the batch file redirecting text and overwriting itself

PAUSE

get1Line.bat
```
@ECHO OFF

FOR /F "tokens=* skip=1" %%i IN (file2.csv) DO ECHO %%i & GOTO next

:next

PAUSE
```

getAnyLineNum.bat
```
@ECHO OFF

REM If line 1 is requested, display it (don't skip any lines)

IF %1==1 FOR /F "tokens=*" %%i IN (file2.csv) DO ECHO %%i & GOTO next

REM Calculate number of lines to skip

SET /A skipVal=%1-1

REM Skip that many lines, display the next line

FOR /F "tokens=* skip=%skipVal%" %%i IN (file2.csv) DO ECHO %%i & GOTO next

:next

PAUSE
```

getColumn3.bat
```
@ECHO OFF

FOR /F "tokens=3 delims=," %%i IN (file2.csv) DO ECHO %%i
```

PAUSE

getData.bat
TITLE %0

HOSTNAME

DIR

PAUSE

getData2.bat
TITLE %0

HOSTNAME

DIR

START doProcess2

PAUSE

getData3.bat
TITLE %0

HOSTNAME

DIR

PAUSE

REM The 'pause' above is only for testing. You would delete it after that.

ECHO.>goAhead.txt

PAUSE

getImageName.bat
@echo off

```
TASKLIST /FO csv| sort>list1.csv

ECHO Open a program, then press enter.

PAUSE>nul

TASKLIST /FO csv| sort>list2.csv

ECHO Delete the other columns in both files, then press enter.

PAUSE>nul

ECHO The difference is:

FC list1.csv list2.csv

PAUSE
```

getLineNum.bat
```
@ECHO OFF

REM Calculate number of lines to skip

SET /A skipVal=%1-1

REM Skip that many lines, display the next line

FOR /F "tokens=* skip=%skipVal%" %%i IN (file2.csv) DO ECHO %%i & GOTO next

:next

PAUSE
```

getValue.bat
```
@ECHO OFF

REM If a value in line 1 is requested, display it (don't skip any lines)
```

```
IF %1==1 FOR /F "tokens=%2 delims=," %%i IN (file2.csv) DO ECHO %%i & GOTO next
```

REM Calculate number of lines to skip

```
SET /A skipVal=%1-1
```

REM Skip that many lines, display the selected value from the next line

```
FOR /F "tokens=%2 skip=%skipVal% delims=," %%i IN (file2.csv) DO ECHO %%i & GOTO next

:next

PAUSE
```

lineReplace1.bat
```
@echo off

SET /P string=%*

ECHO %string:Microsoft=Apple%
```

lineReplace2.bat
```
@echo off

SET /P string=%*

ECHO %string:Microsoft=Apple%>> temp.txt
```

list.bat
```
FOR %%i IN (*) DO ECHO %%i>>list.csv
```

list2.bat
```
FOR %%i IN (*) DO ECHO %%i>>list.csv & ECHO %%i>>list.txt
```

listServices.bat
```
@echo off
```

TASKLIST /FI "SessionName eq Services"

PAUSE

logMe.bat
ECHO %1 ran at %time% on %date%>>log.txt

mainReplace2.bat
@echo off

FOR /F "tokens=*" %%I IN (sysInfo.txt) DO ECHO %%I | CALL lineReplace2

TYPE temp.txt> sysInfo.txt

DEL temp.txt

makeIPs.bat
@echo off

FOR /L %%i IN (101,1,105) DO SET IP%%i=1.2.3.%%i

ECHO IP101=%IP101%

ECHO IP102=%IP102%

ECHO IP103=%IP103%

ECHO IP104=%IP104%

ECHO IP105=%IP105%

PAUSE

raw.bat
FOR %%i IN (*.txt *.csv) DO ECHO %%i>%%i

reverse.bat
@ECHO OFF

```
FOR /F "tokens=1-3 delims=," %%i IN (file2.csv) DO ECHO %%k,%%j,%%i

PAUSE
```

shifter.bat

```
@echo off

SET num=8


:startLoop

        SET var%num%=%8

        SHIFT /8

        SET /A num+=1

IF NOT "%8"=="" GOTO startLoop


ECHO The first 7 parameters are: %1 %2 %3 %4 %5 %6 %7


SET /A num-=1

SETLOCAL ENABLEDELAYEDEXPANSION

FOR /L %%I IN (8,1,%num%) DO ECHO var%%I is !var%%I!

PAUSE
```

top3.bat

```
@ECHO OFF

SET count=0
```

```
SETLOCAL ENABLEDELAYEDEXPANSION
FOR %%i IN (*) DO (
        SET /A count=!count! + 1
        ECHO File!count!: %%i
        IF !count!==3 EXIT /B
)
PAUSE
```

Notes

- **Forfiles** — performs arbitrary cmd on specific file(s) in folder. or subfolders
  can take into account date modified of files.
  can delete, or echo path, etc.

- **%Errorlevel%** — A way to directly recieve output from a function as a 0 or 1. Useful for if/else.

- **SETLOCAL** Enabledelayedexpansion
  used with !ErrorLevel! is useful when dealing with for loops inside if loops etc.

Page 114

Notes

Notes

Notes

Notes

Notes

Notes

Printed in Great Britain
by Amazon